The Legacy of Passion

The Legacy of Passion

Geri G. Cole

authorHOUSE®

AuthorHouse™
1663 Liberty Drive
Bloomington, IN 47403
www.authorhouse.com
Phone: 1-800-839-8640

Published by AuthorHouse   08/28/2012

ISBN: 978-1-4772-6533-8 (sc)
ISBN: 978-1-4772-6534-5 (e)

Library of Congress Control Number: 2012915973

Some names changed for privacy's sake.

The Legacy of Passion

Dedicated

To my children, grandchildren, great grandchildren and all those who will come after them, I leave my legacy of passion.

To Chip, who would rather be called Dan
Thank you for giving up so much of these last years to make my life more comfortable. Thank you for being so sensitive to God's Word and wisdom. Thank you for loving me through these difficult times. Thank you for being God's man.

CONTENTS

INTRODUCTION

Dedicated to those who share my adventure with passion. Look into my heart.

Passion. It's deeper than anything physical. It's controllable . . . . but who would ever want to?

How does it feel? Like your heart is going to explode! It happens in various situations, surrounded by different people, unusual times, and unique circumstances. You never know when it's going to catch you up in the flurry of the moment.

Passion draws you to levels never known or experienced. What's it like?

It thinks differently. It is not restricted to "the norm." When we were told there was no electric power available to us, there was no panic. [There could have been—just married with three little boys, living in a tiny trailer on a clay river bank.] That we were together was all that mattered. We envisioned all kinds of substitutes, but the main thing was, *that was not a problem*. Our passion superceded any "panic."

It's passion that sends you reeling when you find Jesus and become conscious of the fact that He is a real Person. That kind of passion stays with you your whole life as you learn to yield to Him, listen for His direction, and to be still enough to just enjoy His presence. That passion affects how you feel about "church" and "church activities." That passion draws you to seek to please God above and beyond anything else. It gives you peace when everything around you is in disarray. Passion that calls out with ecstasy, "No more! I can hold no more!" when your heart literally feels that it has all it can contain.

Strangely, it's a similar passion that overtakes you when you first hear a grandchild squeal, "Gramma!" or "Grampa!" It's as though the whole core of your being is ready to explode. It's overwhelming. Then each experience with the grandchildren, the great grands, and their parents, takes on new meaning. Your love pours out of you. Sometimes, it is "caught," but not always, and that doesn't matter. The passion you have for your children calls out to intercede for them, to stand in the gap for them when they seem to be straying away. That passion soothes the hurts by young people who don't understand how to respond to those who love them so.

Passion opens the doors for adventures only dreamed about, like racing horseback through a pine forest, experiencing an exhilaration like nothing ever imagined; riding motorcycles through winding mountain roads, the cold wind blowing against your face as you cling to each other. Sailing in the Gulf along the Intercoastal Waterway, stopping at different ports, visiting the tourist shops and enjoying lunch against the backdrop of the harbor. Passion sings as you listen to the splash of waves against the moored craft. The song is heard as the lines slap against the mast, in a harmony only experienced in that time and place. Passion eliminates any thought of discomfort or any mishap and dispels all fears.

It's passion you experience when you find yourself sitting across the room from a man you've grown old with—your eyes meet and your heart skips a beat. You catch your breath and the room full of people suddenly disappears. There you are—just the two of you locked in passion's embrace. He's the one that captured your love forever. Passion held you close and passion has continued through the years. Passion was there when you hurt each other, when you frustrated each other, and passion carried you past all the wounds through to healing.

It was passion that caused a five-foot-long "bird buffet" to be built just outside my family room door so I could watch the birds and squirrels feed. I didn't have the strength to walk across the room, so the feeder was brought close to me. I watched the squirrels and birds share feed, the doves bicker back and forth and the squirrels stretch out with all fours in every direction, their tummies full.

It's passion that allows a couple to talk about the confidential things known only to them. Those very intimate discussions delve into the deepest needs and desires. Passion makes it comfortable, easy to be open and transparent with one another.

The same rush that surged through my whole being when we were young, handsome and vibrant, is there as we care for each other in the weaknesses of aging. It's the passion of a lifetime together.

Most young couples dream of growing old together, of "living happily ever after." But not many arrive at that destination. Most do not. So many do not even comprehend the role that passion plays in our lives. Some just don't recognize it. Others ignore or refuse it. To invite passion into our lives we must learn to be totally open with each other, to allow ourselves to be vulnerable. It means we are willing to expose our deepest longings and personal desires to someone else. It means we trust them enough to protect the things that we dare to share.

It's the only way to live. It is truly, "living life to the fullest," which is the promise made by Jesus. It's what He wants for us. There's a price to pay ~ but it's worth it all.

—Geri G

CHAPTER ONE

"I Thought it was all about *Church!*"

My father had a colorful childhood. I'll tell it the way he did—creatively. He played with the Indian children in Arkansas near the reservation and origin of the Trail of Tears. The Trail of Tears was the name the Indian nations gave the act of "Indian Removal"—a decision by the government when white settlers were demanding l and, and accusing the Indians of being an obstacle. The land was home to the Cherokee, Creek, Choctaw, Chicasaw and Seminole nations. In their travels to the land that the government had chosen and designated for them, many died of hunger, disease, etc.

My father told me my grandmother was an Indian princess. He had all the physical characteristics of Indian heritage, and in fact on his death bed, he needed only a headdress to personify an old chief.

Later, his family moved to Virginia and North Carolina and as a young man he began "ridin' the rails." It was well known during those days that "hobo's" rode [literally] *under* the trains to travel from place to place. They also rode in boxcars, but the term "ridin' the rails" meant that was exactly what they did: they crawled under the train car and laid on the rails of the car.

My father met my mother in Virginia and soon his passion for trains led to him a job with a railroad. My mother was the youngest of a very large family and had a quiet spirit. She was the woman described in that song, "I want a girl just like the girl that married dear old dad." She was a gentle soul and loved by everyone. She lived a simple life, sewing curtains and her own very plain clothes from unbleached muslin. She was my friend. We laughed, shopped, went to movies, and I loved being with her.

They moved to Tampa, Florida and my father worked his way up from a more menial job to that of engineer, which took a lot of study. It seemed as though he was studying the little book of rules for a long time. When we first came to Tampa, we lived near the "train yard" where the engines were brought to the "round house" for repair, etc. It was dirty and loud and thankfully, we didn't have to stay there long. We soon rented a house a few miles away where we lived when my sister, Becky, was born. Finally, we bought a house close to what is now "downtown Tampa." It was an interesting neighborhood. Across the street was a large two-story house with a fence all the way around the block. It was a "Children's Home"—an orphanage. There was no grass, only weeds and I don't remember any outside toys or playground equipment. But then, that was a long time ago. Some of my earliest memories are of seeing the children leaning against the fence, looking out with such despair and hopelessness the little faces are etched in my memory.

My youngest sister, Sandra, was born about that time.

The old frame house had white columns on the porch and windows that slid up and down. They were usually open all summer with warm breezes blowing through the house—in the front door and straight through and out the back door. The wood floors echoed every step and the house felt each jar. My room was on one end of the house and my sisters shared another bedroom.

My little single bed was alongside a window and often, as I lay there waiting to fall asleep, I looked up into the heavens and thought, "God's up there! God, do you see me?" Sometimes, I felt a tug drawing me upward, pulling me out of the center of my little world to a much larger expanse. It didn't take long to realize I could call on God, and somehow, I knew He heard me.

My *interest*—the vest seed of passion—was originally directed toward "church:" *any church I could get to.* In those days, I was there every time the doors were open—Sunday school, Worship service, Vacation Bible School, Christian camp, et.—that was the center of my world. My parents weren't interested for a long time, but that didn't deter the unmistakable pull in my spirit. I had a Sunday school teacher who would take me to Church, and one summer she asked my mother if I could go to Christian camp. The only problem was that I had long hair that my mother braided every morning. The teacher didn't know how to do that, but she promised if I was allowed to go, *she'd learn. I went and she "learned" to braid my hair.* It wasn't the same, but I did get to go to camp.

It was there (wherever "there" was at the time) that I met friends who are still close—some sixty plus years later. We still giggle when we get together and reminisce about the guys that got away, or later in late, the struggles of life's experiences. Forever friends, we're never at a loss for words and most conversations still last into the wee hours of the morning. One long time friend has a "cabin" that her family of four built as the children were growing up. The "cabin" became three stories with a basement, a floor with a high ceiling, kitchen, two bedrooms and a loft with two more bedrooms and bath. It was a favorite place for close friends and ministers. It is an awesome place to get away—if you ever want to "get away."

In the quiet of the early morning, I loved to swing on the second floor porch, and listen to the mountain stream rushing over the rocks below. in the stillness, the sound of heavy trucks crunching the rocks as they climbed the mountain road was the only other sound heard.

Years and years later, as we sat in the big rockers on the balcony of the mountain house, I remember holding my arm out and asking, "What are these wrinkly little lines in my arm?" My friend laughed, "That's old age!!!!!" "Well, yuck!" I squealed, and we giggled just as we had so many years before.

The friends I made in those early years were always the ones who shared my Church life. If I didn't meet them at Church, I soon dragged them along with me. During the teen years, they would come to our house after Sunday night service and I'd make a pot of fudge or some chewy brownies and we'd hang around the piano as I banged out whatever popular tune I'd learned. I became acquainted with a young couple who had three little boys. Some Sunday nights, my friends and I enjoyed going to their house to hang out and enjoy snacks. The young husband was tall, blonde and quite handsome. He was the kind young girls get "crushes" over and I surely did. I married, moved away and back again, and many years later, ran into them. It was as though the years had vanished and we had seen each other the day before. As a young girl, I sat next to the wife in the church choir and learned to sing alto by following along with her. I was an avid student. I loved it.

Years later, as I sang with a worship team at our Church, I watched an older couple hesitatingly walk through the door and down the hall on a Sunday night. As they came in, moving slowly and carefully toward the sanctuary, suddenly I felt a quickening as our spirits witnessed to each other. It was that very same couple with whom I had enjoyed a young girl's crush. The Lord does that for us, you know. Once we meet another believer, our spirits identify one another and we no longer see the outward appearance, but now we recognize the person by their spirit.

What does passion have to do with all that? The passion that grows inside draws you toward certain people. Those people stay close forever. The love you feel for them is not like any other. You know that your relationship is secure and nothing will ever change that. It is passion that carries through the years whether you ever see them or not.

The fervor that locked my spirit to that place called Church was strong. But it was just a touch of all the Lord God had for me. Those early days kept me protected from many of the temptations in the outside world. It was a safe place.

I was twelve years old during a Vacation Bible School "story time" when I realized that just "going to church" was not all there was for me. A group of young students remained in the sanctuary when the little ones were taken to their individual classes for crafts and other activities. The teacher told a story that was touching and revealed a whole new dimension to me. At the end of the story, the speaker said that Jesus loved each one of us and He wanted to come into our hearts and be a part of our lives. With my heart pounding and a whirling in my spirit, I walked down the aisle to her. By then there were tears rolling down my cheeks. When I was told that I could "ask Jesus to come into your heart," I did. the awesome thing about it was that I knew absolutely . . . . *that He did. I called out to Him again. This time, I was certain He heard me.*

There wasn't a big change in my life but it was surely more intense. There wasn't even a hint of the force I would experience in later years. That gentle little seed was slowly developing. There were buds of promise. It was becoming more and more real. It was becoming a part of who I was and who I was to become.

During those young years, I often thought of becoming a missionary and daydreamed about traveling to far away countries to tell strangers about Jesus. Instead, I ran off to Georgia and got married when I was seventeen. It was a wrong decision. At that time, I had not learned the power in saying "No!" *I didn't even know I had that option.* Learning to say "No!" at the right time keeps you from making wrong choices. In fact, learning the empowering of saying "no" will change the very course of your life! That lesson has been a life saver to me many times over the years. One good result from marrying young is that I have three sons from that marriage and I am enjoying my great grandchildren! What an awesome blast is that?!

The delight sown in my spirit during those early years has grown to unbelievable proportions. The warmth and tenderness I experienced in the safety of the Church was a preparation for all the Lord had planned for my life.

Let me reinforce something. The zeal I had for Church, Church people, Church music, Church meetings, Church activities, etc., is *nothing* compared to the passion of actually knowing in the most intimate sense, the Creator of the Universe. The Passion has been directed toward a Person whose name is Jesus. Today, so many years later, the enthusiasm flows from my inner being. The intimacy with Jesus has become the center of who I am. I want you, sweet children, to experience that fervor in its ultimate intensity.

Also, please remember this: I am not talking about religion [Christianity or any other] or Church. I'm talking about au powerfully intimate relationship with a Person, whose name is Jesus.

CHAPTER TWO

Many people have "Passions"

Over the years I have met people who had obsessions that *imitate* passion. They become a counterfeit experience. But those drives are usually self serving. Most of the time, actually. I've known people who have a driving force to "shop" of all things. They not only shop until they drop, they ruin the finances of their families often, and make enemies of their own household. One friend said she hopes there's a Wal-Mart in heaven. I got the impression that if there wasn't . . . . That is very hard for me to understand because basically, *I don't shop*. Others are driven to vices like gambling—and always believe they have a winning—hand, horse, dog, cards, team, etc. They can't even think clearly because their mind is obsessed with "how to get there from here." There are those who are so preoccupied with playing golf, for instance, that they actually *have their home built right on the golf course. Whoops! Is that you?* Golf "enthusiasts" are so passionate about their game, they plan rain or shine, night or day, in the frigid cold of winter or unbelievable heat in the summer. Enthusiastic fishermen are the same way. They are not the least hindered by weather, *they just want to fish*. The desire builds to such an intensity they just can't stand it until they get their line in the water. Ahhhhhhhh, that feels so much better!

There are many who are drawn to the outdoors: fishing, boating, sailing, hunting, tennis, racquetball, gardening, running, walking marathons, bird watching, mountain climbing, etc. Those who hunt spend a lot of time hunting for their dogs. The hunt is centered on the dog's abilities. Some like to watch others play games—hockey, baseball, basketball, tennis, golf, polo, etc. *Puhleeze don't get in their way*. Some derive their excitement vicariously. They watch the excitement of race cars or horses or the expertise of dog or horse training. Many in today's world have a zeal for making money and their lives are spent—night and day—with every thought and thrust toward that goal. They "need" more money. And more money. Is there ever "enough?"

There are those who have a driving compulsion for drugs of all sorts. They are captured by the addiction and only Jesus can set them free. Their lives exemplify the Word of God that explains that the enemy comes to steal, kill and destroy. [John 10:10] But the rest of the verse states that Jesus has come to give us abundant life. Oh, how I wish we could see more people choose Jesus instead of the destructive ways of the enemy. We witness the devastation of families because the father is so obsessed with drugs he won't provide for his family, and, in fact, nothing is more important than that next smoke, fix, or other addictive substance. Of course there are the perverted obsessions. Young men get addicted to Internet and other porn and soon their marriages are overwhelmed. They are incapable of having a healthy relationship, because they have succumbed to the unnatural, unhealthy distortion. They are definitely deceived beyond help in some cases. Our only hope for anyone is Jesus. He's the Healer, the Deliverer, our Savior and He will save anyone who comes to Him. That's His promise.

People with these "strong interests" have a driving force behind them. That obsession is the center of their conversations, and no matter what *you're* talking about, their mind never leaves the subject of their current fascination.

I have a passionate *life*. There isn't much in my life that I am *not* passionate about. I'm just sorry there are so few days in our lives and so few hours in each day. Once I start an oil painting, for instance, I don't want to stop for anything—not laundry, not meal preparation, to clean or study, or any such thing. But then, I'm the same way when I am writing. I don't want to do anything else. I love it. *I'm . . . . passionate about it.*

So what is so different with my own individual passions? The passion I want you to embrace is personal. It is intimate. ***It is possible and it is available to you.***

I truly believe it has to begin with that personal relationship with Jesus because it is "in Him we live and breathe and have our being."

Let me tell you also that passion is not the same as lust. Lust is selfish and only concerned about self gratification—"what's in it for me." *Lust uses people* to get what they want. Passion picks you up and carries you through a roller coaster of infinite adventures.

For twelve years I was a fairly good mother, I think. Well, sometimes I even think I was a fairly good wife. I surely went through the motions. I was thinking today, I remember sitting on the couch with all three of my little sons around me as I read to them. I loved it and I think it instilled in them the passion for study and the joy in finding the adventures in books. I took the boys to Sunday school, to cub scouts, watched their little league games and school programs and was very proud of their efforts. We spent hours with my friend's children and they grew up together even though we lived on opposite coasts of Florida. They all loved the water and we spent a lot of time swimming and picnicking at local campgrounds and parks. When we went to visit the east coast, there was surfing, fishing, and swimming in the ocean. When they came to our house, as they were growing up, we lived on a chicken farm with the smells of burning chickens in addition to the never-ending chicken manure, and millions of flies. We also had horses. But when the east coast children were bored, my friend would just tell them (all four) to sit down and watch the grass grow. (!?)

I loved to cook and prepare unusual meals. I often sewed my own clothes and was a real homemaker. Off and on I worked outside the home, but never for very long. Still, each experience added to the development of who I became. For instance, working for a doctor one summer, I learned an important truth: "The more you learn, the more you will realize how very little you know." Honestly, I don't remember anything else about the job, the office or the doctor. But those words have stayed with me.

During that time, when the boys were young, I became addicted to tranquilizers. I had great difficulty learning to parent the oldest son, who was a curious, energetic and hyperactive little boy. He was a challenge from the time he climbed out of his bassinet. It wasn't long before he was climbing everywhere, including on top of the frig. When I went to our family doctor, he explained, "Take these. We don't know how they work, but nothing will bother you." Nothing [really] did for a long time. We had two boys at the time and they were as different as night and day. David woke up every morning with a smile on his face. He was always happy.

Our third son was born soon after we moved to a new neighborhood in North Tampa. It was a community of young families. The stay at home moms made friends and the children played together as they met from house to house for coffee. In the evenings, they got together at different houses and "partied." There was a lot of drinking in the circle of homes. I drank often until I blacked out. One of those nights, they decided to swap partners. I caught myself just before getting into trouble, and never played that game again. I have to think it was that seed of God in my spirit that stopped me short. The passionate desire to be right with God stayed in my spirit no matter how many mistakes I made, no matter how many wrong choices I made.

We began going to Church as a family. I had taught Sunday school since I was 17 years old, starting with little toddlers, junior girls, teens (my favorite) and young adult women. Growing up in Tampa and moving after marrying, I still found the closest church and always taught a class as soon as I arrived. I loved it then and I still do.

Then I began working "seriously." That is, full time instead of part time. I went to work for a bank and most of the young women there were intellectuals. Or at least they thought they were. They only confused me, talking in circles that each of them seemed to understand. It was just chatter to me. It made me think of people who talk about the theory of evolution as though it were a fact. Not!

Anyone who has ever seen a new born baby, human, bird, mammal or anything from the deepest sea creatures to the most profound land animals, insects, bugs, etc., has to see the intricacies of creation. Perfection. Intimate detail. Only a superior Being could create such variations in every area—colors beyond comprehension, shapes and personalities, diversity in character, size, shape, growth and the reproduction process. There are so many examples—from the species of butterflies to the awesomeness of the salmon, which are spawned in one place, then travel hundreds of miles from there only to return to that very place to spawn their own eggs before they die. How about the way they are obsessed with jumping upstream to make sure they get to the exact place they're supposed to be? With more sophisticated equipment, we are able to see creatures deep in the oceans—unusually beautiful, more colorful that one could imagine. To think that those things "just happened" is absurd.

I have a butterfly story. Actually, I have two. On my trip through Israel with a tour group, I was having intermittent angina attacks and at the time I was also having a lot of trouble with pain in my right knee. It was hard to climb in and out of the tour buses—which we did too many times a day to count. On one day, for whatever the reason, when we boarded the bus, a butterfly flew in as well. It settled on my chest and stayed there. Just stayed there! People talking, making noise, the tour guide chattering away, the bus rolling along, etc. and the butterfly just stayed put on my chest. When we arrived at our next stop, the tiny creature flew out the door and I never saw it again. God has so many ways of letting you know He's there. Right there. Right on your person.

He's going to stay there and make sure you're all right. What makes me think that? Because of the peace that settled in my spirit while it was happening.

The second butterfly story happened right here at home. Following the meeting of a women's group, I walked out to the cars with the girls. One of them noticed a beautiful butterfly perched on a large zinnia blossom. "Get your camera!" everyone squealed at once. Yes, I'm [also] a real camera bug. Well, there was no need to explain that the butterfly wouldn't still be there. So I came inside, got my camera, went back out and—surprise! He was still there! I photographed the lovely creature, and he flew away. I used that lovely photo on a friend's book cover. It still reminds me of both of those butterflies. How can anyone experience such things and not truly believe in a supernatural, creative, God? This God that I know is *personally* interested in every single aspect of your life and mine!

While working with the young women at the bank, I joined them during the lunch break as they put in applications for other jobs. I passed the post office exam and the city civil service exam. One day, an officer from the Tampa police department called me for an interview. They had an opening for—of all things—a police matron!!! Now you've seen the movies where the monstrous and mean matron rules the convicts with an iron hand and booming voice. I surely didn't feel like one of those. I walked into the office and sat down opposite the police officer at the desk. I just thought I'd "go through the motions" of the interview even though I couldn't imagine doing that kind of work. I was 5'5" and weighed about 120. The interviewer made a phone call and shortly a tiny young woman came into the room wearing a blue uniform. The interviewer introduced me to one of the police matrons. Sigh. Okay.

Following the interview, I went back to the bank thinking they would fight to keep me on their payroll. Not! When I told them I could make $100 more a month with the police department, I was wished the best and told if it didn't work out I could always come back to the bank. Well, I gasped. I wondered what on earth the future had in store for me.

Soon I was working from 7 am to 3 pm at the Tampa Police Department. I was now wearing that blue uniform. We changed at the station. Every month we worked a different shift. My tummy never quite got used to one shift before it was time for another. This was totally new to me—I'd never been around policemen, much less prisoners . . . . nor had I ever been exposed to profanity or vulgarity. I will admit the young men on my shift protected me as best they could from the "regulars" who came in fighting, drunk, vulgar and profane. Each matron (female guard) divided their time between the women's jail, and the booking desk. Each four hour shift had its own responsibilities. Each crew included police officers, male guards and matrons. Our own shift was comprised of a variation of personalities and I learned to appreciate each one. Well, most of the time.

When booking the women who had been arrested, I searched them, fingerprinted and photographed them before taking them in the elevator to the second floor jail section. There, I turned them over to the matron working in the jail area. Often they were very drunk and profane. Many times, they were agitated and fighting. Often, they were smelly and very dirty. [I'll not go there.] What a new experience!

It wasn't long before I got well acquainted with those who came in regularly. Mostly they were alcoholics, who got a check the first of the month and as soon as it was used up, they "got arrested" and sobered up in the city jail. That routine was repeated over and over.

It always amazed me to observe the attitude of a person who had been arrested while in the middle of a burglary or following a murder. They would crawl onto a bunk and be asleep in no time.

When working the day shift, we also escorted the women in custody to the city clinic where they were examined every week. *That was interesting.* We also escorted them to court.

I soon needed to pick me up to help me stay awake during those long night shifts. I managed to get prescriptions for them and then began the roller coaster of sleeping pills during the day and amphetamine at night to stay awake. One day, on the way home, I decided to take the sleeping pills. I slid into a hot bath as soon as I got inside the house. I fell asleep in the tub and a tornado passed through my neighborhood while I slept. I learned about it later. I was in serious trouble.

CHAPTER THREE

A Jailbreak

One day, a message came for one of the police officers who worked in the Identification Section (fingerprints and photography). His little four year old son was dead on arrival at a nearby hospital.

I gave him the call and then didn't see the officer again for a while and didn't learn many of the details except that the little boy was riding a tricycle in the family room when he fell over dead. They took him immediately to the hospital but he never recovered.

When I had been working at the police department for about three and a half years, I was sleeping one day when there was a loud knock on the door. Standing before me was a very "official looking" man in a dark suit with papers in his hand. He was there to advise me that our house was facing foreclosure. The mortgage payments hadn't been made in months. What a shock! I was under the impression that as a dutiful wife, when I turned my paycheck over to my husband and *trusted* him to pay the bills, I didn't need to be concerned any further. Not! Needless to say, that was *upsetting to say the least*. Within a few days, I woke up to a phone call telling me that my loan payment was overdue. *Well, I didn't know I had a loan payment*. But later I learned that my husband had a gambling habit. I began to put two and two together. My typewriter and other things disappeared that I later learned were pawned for gambling money.

The following Friday, when I got my paycheck, I made the decision to hold on to it for a change. When asked for it, I just explained that the children had needs: shoes, coats, etc. *And I kept the money*. I was scared to death. I don't even know why. For me, with my background, that just wasn't anything I would ever do. But I did. The following Sunday we celebrated my sister's anniversary at our house. As we sat around the table, out of the corner of my eye I saw my husband walk toward the door with his clothes over his shoulder.

"What are you doing?" I asked. I was dumbfounded.

"I'm leaving." He answered, still walking. All I could think of was that he was leaving me because I dared to keep my paycheck. My mind whirled. After that, much of what happened was a blur.

I don't know what I expected, but this was not it. At that point, the mortgage was already in arrears and loan companies were constantly calling or sending their "reminders." Soon I had more shocks. Because a car we had bought had my name on the loan, the payment was deducted from my bank account. Then checks I had written began to bounce. This had never happened to me before. Suddenly my life was turned upside down! Then my car was repossessed. The window air conditioner was picked up, in addition to the lawn mower, and so many things that had been bought on credit—and then not paid for. We had recently purchased a new freezer. Yep, that went too.

While all that was going on, I had also lost my sitter because of the new shifts I was working. My friend down the street who had been caring for them couldn't keep them overnight. A friend who had lived across the street from me now lived in Miami, but she came all the way to Tampa to stay with my boys as long as I needed her. By that time, my life was a rollercoaster.

My husband began calling me at work wanting to come back home. I never told him to leave so it only seemed right for him to move back. He did, and my friend returned to Miami. But there was an attitude that I couldn't deal with. After my crying for three or four days, he moved out for good. So I searched out a live-in nanny.

That only caused a new set of events. The nanny was great but by now the boys were suffering their own turmoil. This was a new world for me. I just simply didn't know what to do about anything. One day the nanny called and said the older boy was on the roof and she couldn't get him to come down. Another time, one of the boys had started a fire in their clothes closet. There was some kind of "acting out" going on most of the time. Then my husband began calling again at all hours of the day and night.

Since I didn't have transportation to work [the car had been repossessed], I was taking the bus from the police department in downtown Tampa sometimes as late as 11:30 at night. My parents had a second car but they wouldn't let me use it . . . .

One day a man was arrested that was well known to the officers on my shift. They all greeted each other and talked like old friends when he came in, handcuffed and grinning. He had bragged that there wasn't a jail that could hold him. So the officers were smug when he came in. "Well, Larry, looks like we've got you beat this time!" they taunted confidently.

Now this police station was new and had been publicized as completely secure, so they had every reason to feel confident in holding him. In a few days, his girlfriend was arrested and placed in the female jail. But it wasn't long before—just days actually—Larry broke out of the jail and took the jail keys with him! [They were very large keys—about five inches long—and painted bright colors, not easily hidden!]

I'll never forget that day. Pure bedlam broke out. The officers who knew him were furious. They had a lot of anger, anyway. After the flurry and panic of the breakout was settled and a new routine was in place, officers from the Selective Enforcement Unit were assigned to the female jail to keep Larry from breaking his girlfriend out. At that point, they didn't put anything past him. The female jail had an outside corridor surrounding the jail area and an SEU officer was assigned to patrol that area every shift.

The officer assigned to my shift was the man whose son had died. He was tall and somber. He was what you would call a "quiet presence." We got a change to get acquainted during the midnight shift. He came into the matron's office in the jail section for coffee and we talked. He warned me about some of the mistakes I was making—like leaving jail doors open . . . He was very protective and that was a new experience for me.

On those long midnights, I learned we had gone to the same high school, but never met. As teens we lived in the same neighborhood, walked the same route to school, but never met. We even had some of the same friends . . . . Then we both married and he and his wife lived one block north of me and my good friend babysat his children. After his little boy died, he and his wife separated. He was now living with his parents. I talked to him about be a Christian. Something in our spirits connected.

But remember, *my whole concept* of being a "Christian" was to go to Church. Naturally, my suggestion to him was to find a good church and . . . . *just goes there*. I gave him a Bible and he took it with him. At one service, the pastor preached about Saul, the Jew who had been so cruel to the early Christians. Saul led soldiers to drag the new believers out of their homes, and take them to prison or worse. Many of the new believers were thrown to the wild animals *for sport*. It is said that Nero used Christians as lights in his gardens. Dipped in tar, they burned for his pleasure.

Dan had always had contempt for Christians and was quick to express his opinions. But when he heard the story about Saul, who brought about such atrocities to God's people, he listened intently. You see, Saul was very religious and he really thought he was doing God a favor. After he heard the story of Saul, Dan went home and laid across his bed with the Bible on the floor. He went through many pages before he found Saul's story. Saul wasn't look for God, instead, Jesus came to him, and that was after His ascension to Heaven! Jesus' words were, 'Saul, Saul, why are you persecuting *Me?*" [When we criticize God's people, make judgments against them, we are actually pointing a critical finger at God's son!] As Dan read, the Holy Spirit quickened in him that God loved him even though he had not loved His people. Dan was broken in his spirit and he asked Jesus to save him. And He did. The next week, he invited me to come to his water baptism, being held at the church hear his home. I took my little boys and witnessed his baptism. Our lives would never be the same, but we had no comprehension of the magnificent plan God had for us . . . . together. The next step Dan took was to begin reading the Bible. He began with Matthew and was shocked at what he learned. From the beginning, he trusted the Word of God and he obeyed it. But then, he ran into a glitch.

CHAPTER FOUR

Waves of Sweet Memories

Watching the ebb and flow of the ocean waves reminds me of the way our memories suddenly rush into our spirits. Just sitting quietly, we experience the tender reminder of some sweet time. Like the breaker against the shore slowly seeps into the sandy beach and quietly disappears, we take a deep breath and our thoughts move on to the activity at hand. Over and again those stories of the past surface, at different times and seasons, some raging high in the midst of our minds, then rushing in to bring the burst of passion, the tenderness of romance and the stillness of promises kept. Let me share some of those as they flow quietly in my spirit.

On this particular morning, the floor was strewn with cardboard boxes, some packed and labeled, ready for mailing, some half-filled, with supplies to be sent to Kenya: dry milk, rice, oil, sweet cereals, flour, everything they needed right then. A battered violin case leaned against the wall, holding reminiscences of hours of practice and leaving a mother's wishes of concert halls to the joy of learning to play gospel music by eat on the guitar . . . . In the next room, the crackling sound of damp firewood broke the stillness of the early morning—a rare winter dawn in Florida—cold enough to start a fire. The temperature was all of 40 degrees and sure to be 70 degrees by the afternoon. We grabbed every chance to enjoy the fireplace.

Instrumental worship music soon filled the room and we danced in the darkness of daybreak. This gentle giant of a man held me close. His arms wrapped me in a safety I had come to appreciate in our later years. The richness of Beethoven provided the setting as we moved with its intensity. The fullness of God's overwhelming creation filled his eyes and my heart. Not unusual. My husband of over forty years was always touched by God's creation, especially in music. With his eyes filled the tears, his love flowed from h is spirit to mine and I understood what John Sanford explained in one of his many books on marriage and relationships. When God's Word says we'll be "one," I never really comprehended it. Yet, we reached that point, where our spirits flowed back and forth, as we learned to yield to one another. With a backdrop of a full bookcase, the wide span of our interests was discovered. Manuals on marine navigation, Florida gardening and pest control, Bibles and references, model airplanes, their construction and instruction on flying them, were near the books on analysis of personalities, the power of love and forgiveness, and other materials from which we had drawn over the years. A variety of interests were haphazardly placed: A discussion of the Dead Sea Scrolls was now propped up alongside "Splashes of Joy in the Cesspools of Life," [(c) 1992] by Barbara Johnson.

What a glorious conception: music in all its forms came from the heart of a God who loved all the various sounds, all the compositions and overtures. It was by His hand that He fashioned in the minds of men instruments made from every source of wood, metal, skins, etc. He spoke variations of musical notes into the ears of listening men and women who were sensitive to His voice. Many never knew the Voice, but they heard and created anyway, and people were moved beyond comprehension at His marvelous gift. Compositions came from the creative force of God's Spirit and it continues to flow to listening ears and hearts and minds today. Some are moved to tears at the expression of His love as it emanates from the various instruments. The power of overtures fills the sensitive heart to overflowing joy. *Music encompasses all forms of passion.*

I'll never forget the first touch—alone and now knowing each other—as our arms brushed against each other. Just a touch, but never to be forgotten. We had grown up near each other, but no matter how close we lived, how many mutual friends we had, we never met. Years, marriages, children and divorces later, our arms touched in an elevator of the Tampa Police Station as we went about our separate duties. He was a police officer and I worked as a police matron in the Booking Desk and women's jail. He was tall, quiet and carried himself in a mature but humble spirit. In his uniform, he commanded respect, but there was more than a uniform that brought respect. He was an esteemed officer, who was polite, fair and courteous. No vulgarity, no profanity, nothing about him was disrespectful in any way *to anyone.*

Long after my childhood with father, mother and two sisters, after a disappointing marriage that left me devastated and disoriented, on this night I as sitting at a table in a Spanish restaurant with all the amenities of Ybor City's finest Cuban cuisine. In the flair of Spanish décor, I became a part of a surreal scene as violinists strolled over and played. I've seen too many movies, I thought. But no, as they played softly, a guitarist joined them. I sat across from a young man in a white dinner jacket. His long legs and quiet spirit opened the door to a new world where everything was distinctively unique. *Everything was romantic.*

Warm kisses over breakfast after a long and difficult midnight shift was a little too much for the proprietor who [not so politely] asked us to leave. Sigh. The world disappears and there are only the two of you. That first passion as deep desires to hold one another, to touch, and to melt into the gaze of love that draws you together.

I'd never been on a motorcycle before, but I had no fear. Sitting behind him, I held on tightly and felt our hearts beat together. It was no surprise when we had *that experience.* One day, he took me for a ride on his a Norton 750. He decided to take a short cut through a pasture to show me a half acre of property he was buying. It was on a Creek that curved through the virgin forest until it emptied into the Hillsborough River. That became the location for our first home. The ground was thick red clay, where everything grew—vegetables, chickens, rabbits, ducks, possums, snakes, etc. It was near impossible to watch the boy's tough jeans—scrubbed in the bathtub because there was no electricity—no water, except that from the Creek, which had to be carried up the slippery clay bank by the bucketsful.

The power company told us there was no access for the property which was too far away from the closest power lines. No electricity? No problem. We'd manage. That's the way passion thinks.

Sometimes, people look at us and want to ask, "Don't you even understand the problem?" No, there *was no problem* as long as we were together. At that time, nothing else really mattered.

I had never lived "on the land." [Actually, I didn't know what the term meant!] Never grew vegetables, and heavens!—*never picked eggs or watched a hog being slaughtered. Nope. All new experiences. All because of passion. Passion picked me up and sat me down in a world where dreams come true, some before you have the chance to dream them! Passion opens the door.*

Early in our marriage we raced horseback through a pine forest, and with the wind in my face, exhilaration beyond expression filled my spirit with overflowing joy. Dan rode his stallion, Red Feather, a Tennessee Walker and I rode Blaze, the Morgan, who was strong and rode hard, especially heading toward home. When my gallant steed took a left and I kept going forward, it was passion that caused me to land in elated ecstasy.

I'd never flown anywhere, so when the opportunity to go to Alaska was presented, it was a no brainer. Two weeks away from each other opened the door to a refreshingly new and passionate welcome. A breathtaking two weeks was more than any commercially planned honeymoon. We stayed on base, and our time was our own. Exhilarating kisses, brisk walks on the dry cold mornings and fresh clean air were brand new experiences. We took deep breaths as though we could keep them forever. A far cry from the hot, humid Florida summer.

I had never been out of the country, so when I got a call from my long time friend offering the excursion to Israel, I had but one thought: Dan will never agree to it. I was having a lot of angina, my knees were painful, and I was frequently short of breath. The first step was to pray, "Lord this is an amazing offer. I'll know it's your plan if Dan is agreeable." He shocked me by agreeing almost immediately. Part of the ease in which he made that decision was that my friend was a nurse. Almost immediately, she called to say the lady who was scheduled to be my roommate had cancelled. She asked if I could find someone who would be able to take the trip and room with me. A good friend went through the same thing, asking her husband, who would be left alone, and he, too, immediately gave his consent and encouraged her. So we found ourselves flying to Israel, and in my case, it was completely paid for. I knew God had something up His sleeve. What was this all about? We rode tour buses, were given more information and history than I could possibly absorb, and climbed up and down the steps until my poor legs screamed in agony at the end of the day. Then one day the tour guide decided to take the whole busload to her mothers home for a visit. What a gracious and unexpected blessing.

We've had a home fellowship meeting for our thirty years. We share a meal and then gather around our family room as Dan plays the guitar as we sing together. We did that every week for thirty years. On one night, our eyes met and my heart began to pound. A joy welled up and I couldn't help but smile as I caught my breath. While locked into that gaze, the room full of people disappeared and the love and tenderness we felt for each other melted like warm oil that flowed over my whole being. We were in our seventies and the passion was still alive.

On a visit to my son's house about an hour north of where I live, I experienced a new kind of delight. When the door opened, my little granddaughter squealed, "Gramma!" and I thought the core of my being would explode. Never in my whole life had I felt my heart so full of love

17

and it was wrapped up in this tiny little person. It's been said that if we had known what joy our grandchildren would bring, we'd have had them first. Oh, yeah!!!! Amen!

Riding close behind him on the Harley, holding on with all my might, we rode through the winding mountain roads of North Georgia. I thought, "Here we go! Another tender adventure in loving. There's surely nothing like this." I felt his strength that was passion at its ultimate. The cold mountain air caught us off guard after leaving Florida's heat and humidity not many hours earlier. We had no concept of the extreme changes in temperature in what seemed a very short time and distance. The winding roads leading to the mountains of North Georgia were fun to travel. The higher we were, the cooler the temperature and the longer it took to get where we were going. Another new lesson.

While on a Divinely planned trip to Alaska, the Lord gave us all kinds of unusually overwhelming experiences. Picking blueberries on the side of the mountain with my two young sons was surely an event wild and unheard of in this new world of adventure. Passion opens the door to untold encounters, opening our eyes and hearts to all His magnificent and glorious world. "Look here!" He'd whisper. "Hey, don't miss this!" I'd hear deep within my spirit. It was a new world to these flatlanders. There were very few roads in and out of Anchorage at that time, and when we stopped at a bait shop, I was surprised to learn that we had to hike quite a distance to the lake. I tried my best to be open and aware of everything in every direction. Like watching the flip flop salmon splashing their way to the spawning ground. The rules for fishing for salmon were unusual. Different colors for different days. They wee so thick, we could easily have walked into the shallow water and picked the one we wanted. But we were required to catch them with a hook and line. They were easily snagged. When the line accidentally did snag one, Dan had to go out into the water, release the hook and try again!

Standing high in the mountains of Alaska, looking down over the peaks and experiencing the presence of clouds gently floating by, I was ready to break out in song. It was a scene right out of "Sound of Music." This new life was exceedingly above and beyond my wildest comprehension. What on earth would happen next?

Years later, not at all well, I was unable to walk across the room without shortness of breath and pain, so Dan built a five foot long "bird buffet" just outside the glass door so I could watch the multitude of wild birds and squirrels as they came to munch the select morsels provided for them. Passionate love is creative and it's always thinking of ways to please the one you love. Dan anticipated my every need and desire. He spoiled me and I loved it.

"Do it again, Gramma! Do it again!" my little granddaughter giggled, as I splashed her up and down in the swimming pool. The biggest "rush" was in my own being. How can so much love be packed into such a tiny little person? So precious. So tender. So sweet.

We love to go out on the Gulf. Dan was passionate about fishing and he was quite good at it (of course) and I loved the ride. I'd take a book or two, some snacks, and while he fished, I'd munch. The silence was interrupted only by the lines slapping against the mast. But once, when we were in a power boat and were quite a distance out in the Gulf, far from the sight of land, the engine broke down. Why did I have such peace? I had complete and utter confidence in my husband's capacity to fix anything. I felt completely safe and secure in his ability to get me to safety. Not to worry. Not to fret. Not to become anxious. Passion can bring peace. Of course he found the problem and repaired it with something we had on the boat. He knew hot to "make do" with just about anything. What really bothered me, was that he had a *spare* of just about everything . . . .

Over a hundred pansies—planted along the sidewalk to our front door. "And every one says, 'I love you." Incredible words, even in our 60's.

On the way to another bird feeder that he had built outside my office window, I noticed that when I wasn't looking, he had planted some wild flowers along the path I took around the side of the house. Why does that stir my heart? Passion causes your heart to fill to overflowing, to appreciate every gesture of love.

Early in my life, the tiny seed of passion was planted in my young spirit. No one in my family seemed to understand. Maybe they didn't even notice! I had a longing toward God—expressing itself in attendance at the nearest Church. There was peace and contentment there. Was it the preaching? The music? The friends I met? I don't remember much of anything except for the enthusiasm that drew me *to that place*. We didn't relocate often, but when we did, I quickly searched out the nearest house of worship.

The Lord drew me to Himself and that's how the passion began in my life. Since then, I've met many people, and through the years, I've discovered that "passion" in itself is rare. So many people live their whole lives with no thrust, no excitement, and no enthusiastic interest in anything but the mundane day to day life. How sad. Why is it?

I want to tell you how this ardent energy has developed over the years, taking me to worlds unknown, to experiences beyond my wildest dreams or imagination. Come, let's explore. Let's see if we can encourage others to take this thrilling journey!

Chapter Five

God Has a Ways and Means Committee

Back to the jail experiences. After a period of time, Larry's [the guy who escaped our jail] girlfriend was transferred to another detention center and the SEU officers were relieved of their responsibilities to the female jail. The officer I had gotten to know still worked the same shifts. He had returned to the Identification Section, and we got to see each other often. Sometimes he was assigned to the booking desk, where I worked part of the shift. When a woman came in screaming obscenities and fighting, he would suddenly appear out of nowhere and just "be there." The righting would end abruptly.

The matrons and guards worked four hours in the Booking Desk and four hours in the jail. The elevator was locked and after searching the prisoner, we transported them to the jail area. That's where I had my first "encounter" with the passionate "rush" between me and "that young police officer." "*Alone in the elevator with him and the female prisoner, my arm brushed his and something like an electric shock ignited my whole system. I felt a "rush" surge through my being.*" "Yes, it was Dan.

We got off the midnight shift, changed out of our uniforms and walked out the door at the same time. The morning air was brisk and clean—in comparison to the odors of the jail, etc. I took a deep drink of that early morning atmosphere and looked up at him. "Want to go to breakfast?" Dan Asked. Sure. Usually, I was ready to rush home and get some sleep, but *somehow*, this seemed like an excellent idea. And that was just the beginning.

One day, Dan invited me to take a ride on his 750 cc Norton motorcycle to see some property he was buying. Another new adventure for me! I had never been on a motorcycle at all! We rode north of the city to a wooded area. When we came to a pasture, he turned and continued to drive right through the mucky wet ground. **Get this picture! The ground was soggy from heavy downpours in the previous week. This was pasture—cow pasture with all that goes with "pasture." It was only a few minutes of slipping and sliding in the deep, mushy, sod when the motorcycle got stuck.** It just dug its way into the mess and stopped.

Dan, asking for help very kind, said, "Geri, just get behind it and push." I think "passion" had already clicked in, because I never even *considered* the consequences. I got behind the bike, up close and personal, grabbed the seat . . . and pushed as hard as I could. The bike pulled out, propelling the wet and sour, gushy grassy mud all over me including my face. It propelled me backward and I splashed down hard in the much. We laughed. Dan tried to pull me up but instead, joined me. We scraped the mud off and drove the three miles deep into the wooded area. The plot was far from "the main road," down a dirt path, across a rickety wooden bridge and through the virgin forest. The property was on the bank of a creek of cold fresh water that that flowed into the Hillsborough River. The ground was red clay. There was nothing there but ground, but he loved the idea of being right on the water. While we were walking around, a neighbor strolled over with a very visible gun secured in a shoulder holster and high boots. (That's not all; he had other clothes on, too!) I stared and he stared right back. We must have been some sight!

He quickly explained, "Lookin for snakes. They come around when it's wet like this." Thanks. That really was "too much information."

Dan and I spent time together and I mentioned the different things that had been repossessed when my husband left me. He was quick to suggest some alternatives.

"Well, can you afford a second-hand washer?" he asked. Second-hand? I had never ever bought anything second-hand. I bought everything new, and on credit. Monthly payments, and unable to pay those.

"Sure," he explained. "You could probably get one for little or nothing. Maybe as little as $25," he explained. Here we were in never-never land again. Never been her nor done that. "I'll go with you and help you find one," he said. I was shocked that all those years we were in debt when we could just as easily have bought and paid for the things we needed by paying cash *for something second-hand.*

So, little by little, "things" were replaced. I kept my job, got an older car and proceeded on with my new life.

I took the boys out to the Christian Campgrounds one day for a picnic. Across the lake, I saw Dan swimming toward us. He swam all the way across the rather large lake then he shared our picnic. The boys played in the wooded area—the oldest picked up a rather large gopher turtle. The middle son tried to catch a little rabbit, but he got away. We just had a great time together, and I thought, "This has go to be the ultimate perfection." I was deliriously happy but of course the boys were not. No matter what the situation is, children are the losers and parents separate. Often, they think it's their fault and I didn't have the wisdom to know how to talk to them.

I dated Dan Cole. We began going to church together and (of course) I started teaching a Sunday school class. Dan taught a boy's class and also was active in a scout type boys group. We went on "visitation" together and met a lot of people. The boys were active in the children's activities. It felt good. It felt *right.*

We shared coffee at the police cafeteria, and talked at the booking desk or in the women's jail, when he accompanied the matron delivering a new prisoner. We talked on the phone. I remember one evening during a heavy rain storm. Dan called and said he was talking on a phone from a telephone booth. Dan began to ask me questions about the things he was reading in the Bible. I didn't have any answers. Remember, my *"connection" was with the Church.* On the phone one evening, he commented that God had "told him . . ." Well, that was very new to me! *How [or why?] did God talk to him?* I had been a Christian since I was 12 years old and *God never talked to me!!* More than that, I had never met anyone else who had *personally* heard from God.

"Just ask Him a question and then, listen," he explained very simply. Well I did. I sat on the edge of my bed and waited for an answer. I waited and waited some more. I heard nothing. I gave it up. I realized that Dan had entered a place I had never been, and he was learning so much about the Bible! Remember, I had been "teaching" in the church most of my life. It was the same Bible, but now, *I had met someone who really took it seriously.* When, in God's Word, He said to forgive everyone no matter how they treated you, Dan believed it and took it to heart. When it warned about retaliation, it was burned into his spirit. I had never met *anyone* who too the Bible *that earnestly.*

On our first "real date," Dan arrived at the door in a white dinner jacket and I looked quickly to see if there was a horse drawn carriage outside. It was like a dream. He took me to a Spanish Restaurant where violinists and guitarist strolled among the tables. It was delicious. It was breathtaking. It was just like the fairy tales and I thought about those 'happily ever after" endings.

He rowed up into the shallows of the Hillsborough River, and I picked water lilies on the way. We stopped and had a picnic at the water's edge. There was a canopy of lush spring leaves overhead. Every experience was new, taking my breath away. The clear water of the river flowed quietly and the little boat headed away from the wide open water as the river narrowed. It was a dream, surely.

Passion flows out of your inner being and covers your countenance. Everywhere we went, people stared. The smiles on our faces just wouldn't go away. One day when we were out, Dan just picked me up and twirled me around. With both of us grinning from ear to ear, we were quite the spectacle. A warm, fuzzy, spectacle. We were deliriously happy with each other but at the same time there were many things happening in our lives that were hurtful, frustrating and disturbing. No need to "go there" right now.

We began spending more time with the boys and I thought this was a relationship made in heaven. But children don't think that way and these little boys were no different. I was too much in love to even recognize the signals they were sending out and they were sending plenty of them.

At Thanksgiving, Dan came to dinner at my folk's house, but my father was quite open about not liking police officers. "It takes a thief to catch a thief," was his critical remark.

During this time, the children's father had visitation with them on weekends. They were usually so emotionally cold when they returned home, I suspected that their father was turning them against me. Fifty years or more, later, however, I learned that they were simply traumatized (naturally). Divorce doesn't make any sense to children. We never fought, there were no "scenes" in the home. When they were with me, they resisted Dan being there. When they were with their dad, they were hurt that he had a girlfriend. There is nothing "natural" about divorce, and especially when there are children. That is why the Lord actually said He hated divorce. [Malachi 2:16]

Dan continued his study of the Bible. One evening we went to dinner. He looked at me seriously and said, "You know the Bible is against marrying a divorced person. We haven't talked about marriage, but I know now how God feels about it, and I think we need to stop seeing each other."

I was shocked. I was crushed. I was devastated. The joy and excitement rushed from my spirit and depression engulfed me. There was no argument since he was "minding God." Of course, I tried to out guess him. I had question after question rolling around in my mind. I was obsessed with the hurt and we still worked in the same place. We saw each other almost every day. Every time I saw him, I ached all over. My heart felt like it was surely breaking. Now, there were no kisses in the elevator, no hugs when we met after work, no love notes sent through the pneumatic tubes. As passionately as he loved me, he loved the Lord more. A friend once told me, "Most Christian women just want a husband who loves Jesus more than they do." I believe that. I had found one.

I went to work, prepared meals, did laundry, watched the children's plays, softball games, all the while empty, hurt, and paralyzed with fear of the unknown. I don't know how long that period lasted, but *it was too long for me.*

Then I received a phone call from Dan. "Geri, I was washing my motorcycle today when suddenly the Lord spoke to me," he began. "As clearly as I hear you now, I heard Him say, 'Your love is true and your purpose is Mine.' That's all; and at once a surreal peace came over me. I knew what God said about divorce and marrying a divorced person. But now I looked at divorce as sin, and I knew sin could be forgiven."

"What does that mean for us?" I asked, holding my breath in anticipation of the answer.

"I think it means we'd better be mighty sure of our relationship, putting Him first in everything, and acknowledging the sin of divorce." He answered.

I could hardly wait. My heart pounded when I saw him from a distance, and I couldn't contain my exhilaration. He held me and I felt the kind of peace that exudes protection, safety, security and shelter. In his arms I had found a place of security.

Immediately, he made a covenant with God and wrote it down. It read:

Dear Lord, Our Covenant

We have trusted Thee as our Savior, Dear Lord
We now and forever, with Thy help, yield ourselves fully unto Thy service.
We devote, with deepest loyalty, our every thought to Thy doctrine.
We acknowledge that because of our sin, our task is tremendous.
We praise Thee, Dear Lord, with love in our hearts for Thee.
We promise, that our lips and our hearts be devoted to Thy Service.

Our Prayer

Dear Lord, is that our every moment reflect the good of Thy Way.
That each soul our path doth cross, feel Why warmth in us.
That we are used by Thee, Dear Lord, to quicken the salvation of lost souls.
That we are ever vigilant in the guidance of our children, so they may also know the blessings of
Thy Way.
We ask Thine assistance in safeguarding their spiritual and physical health and well being,
That Thy most heartfelt compassion manifests in the hearts of those who dwell in the home.
We completely dedicate our abode, what and wherever to Thy Honor . . .

The theme of our life having been found within Thy Book
"And we know that all things work together for good to them that love God, to them who are
the called according to His purpose." [Romans 8:28]

Our Answer—"Your love is true, your purpose is Mine."

This had hung in our house for over 40 years.

CHAPTER SIX

New Beginnings

Dan took me to dinner one evening and as he prayed over the meal, holding my hands, he slipped a ring on my finger. I felt it. I knew what it meant. My heart pounded in anticipation. I opened my eyes just as he was saying, "Will you? Will you marry me?" Oh!!! My heart was already overflowing and now, there was a decision. We would marry.

Dan and I looked for a trailer to put on his land and found a second hand one—of course—that was very small: 41' by 8'. I was currently working on a quilt and Dan set up a tent and covered the ground so that I could sit cross legged and finish the tiny quilting stitches. There were bunk beds for the boys and a bedroom at the end for us. He had it pulled onto the property and then started making arrangements for power, water, and the essentials. But the power company said there was no way we could bring electricity to that area. I don't remember why, but that was the final word: "NO!"

No electricity? No problem. We'd manage. That's the way passion thinks. We began to consider the ways we could "manage." We had lots of ideas. We were not the least concerned. Water? At first we began carrying water from the creek. That meant carefully crawling down the slippery clay bank with a container, filling it, then climbing back up to get it in the trailer—for flushing, etc. It was an adventure each time we went out to Trout Creek. *A real adventure.*

Dan's friend from the Records and Identification section brought his truck, and he and Dan used it to dig a well. It was pure ecstasy see that first water flow when we pumped it by hand. It smelled like rotten eggs, and tasted like sulphur, but once it was boiled, you *hardly even noticed it. Then we all worked on digging the septic tank drainage lines.*

Suddenly—with no announcement or warning—the power company approved the property for electricity. It's amazing how much you learn to appreciate the simplest things when you don't have them. Preparations were being readied for our move. The wedding date was getting closer and closer, and we were spending more and more time working on the property.

The day of the wedding arrived along with a downpour. On the way to the Church, Dan saw a car disabled with a flat tire. Yes, he got out and changed the tire in the rain. But the wedding took place and the dream I had that I could actually wake up with him beside me was really going to happen. That's the "happily ever after" part I longed for.

Surprisingly for me, there was quite an adjustment in bringing these little city boys to the virgin forest. They explored deep into the woods, found all kinds of exciting things like a small pond with fish. They saw deer, a panther, and numerous other wild animals. Dan taught us to "try everything" so we ate rattlesnake, wild rabbits, armadillos, possums, turtles, and whatever they found. Dan taught them to do so many things. I really thought this was a perfect situation: to have the boys grow up in the woods. The creek was full of fish and alligators. We could see the alligator's little pink eyes bouncing along the water's surface at night.

With all the positive things that I saw, those little boys were still hurting. *You can't make anyone love you.* The boys tried Dan's patience. He found out how short his "fuse" was. Often, he would just drive off when he realized his anger was getting out of hand. That was a new experience for me. He wouldn't say anything, just . . . drive off. As much as we talked *before the wedding*, now we couldn't seem to communicate at all. Then something happened to James that caused him to want to leave there as soon as possible. He continued to plead with me and in just a short time after we were married, he went to live with his father. It was years later that I learned what that was all about and by then there had been much damage.

Things were not so good at his father's house, either. His dad married a *much younger woman*, not much older than him, and he was so enraged, he began climbing out the window at night. He quickly met the wrong crowd, and while riding someone's motorbike, he had an accident that did irreparable damage to his leg.

I abandoned him. No excuses. He lived with his dad and I distanced myself from them—selfishly. Thinking *only* of myself, I left him alone. I think he spent many years pursuing a mother figure. I hurt him physically and emotionally. There is no excuse, but that is the reality. I'm sharing this because I know I am not *now* that person. But during that period of my life, *I was that person and my son suffered the results and kept the scars from those years.*

Dan had his own traumatic experience. While mowing the "yard" with a push mower, he yanked on the "pulley," which slipped out of his hands. The wooden end went flying, and whipped Dan's leg several times hard. But the skin wasn't broken, so he never thought anything about it except that it was *really sore*.

One night, sitting at his desk at the police station, he smelled something, and when he examined his leg, he saw that it was open and looked terrible. The next day we went to my old family doctor. That was definitely God's direction, because he told us if his son, a surgeon, had seen that gangrenous would, he would have immediately amputated his leg. The doctor treated it ever day for a long time, and finally he turned the nursing over to me. Amazingly, the leg was saved. Our God is an awesome God. Dan lived to be 72 years old and even though he had some circulation problems along the way, he died with his leg intact.

As we look back over our lives, we realize we are different people at the various times. The Bible gives us an example in Jacob's life. He was born a supplanter, cheating his brother out of his birthright, lying to his father. Then he fought with an angel all night and was given the name, "Israel." After that night of wrestling, he was left with his hip out of joint. [My friend tells me she doesn't trust anyone who doesn't walk with a limp!] At the end of his life, Jacob became the fruit of God's promise to Isaac, his father, and Abraham, his grandfather. He was the same man, but he was being changed as God dealt with him throughout his life. When we think of our lives, and the changes God makes as we yield to His direction and brings us *through* situations, we too, become different people. God's Word says that when we are "in Him, old things pass away and behold all things become new!" [II Cor 5:17] Dan said [at least once] that the reason the phrase, "And it came to pass" is repeated so many times in the Scripture is that *everything comes to pass and nothing comes to stay.* Isn't that encouraging?

It's interesting that when that seed of passion is planted deep within, even though it might lie dormant for periods of time, it's still there, and it will still produce fruit. My life is proof.

Daily existence was challenging at Trout Creek. But from my ["blind love"] perspective, it was great for the boys. Dan worked midnights, and before he left for work in the evening, he'd take David and some trot lines and go out to the river and drop them in. The "trot lines" were made of gallon bleach bottles, with lines tied to them. On the lines were several baited fish hooks. When he came from work the next morning, he'd check the trot lines and almost always bring home fish: catfish especially, and sometimes a turtle. I learned an excellent recipe—dipping the catfish fillets in egg, then potato flakes before frying them. It was a delicious blend of catfish and hash browns, all in one.

One of the most difficult and challenging experiences was digging. *Everything we did needed a hole to be dug!* We thanked God that we were allowed to put in a power pole. But then, there was the digging. Picture the "digging:" the shovel or post hole digger had to be shoved into the clay ground, the lifted out of the hole, the clay scraped off the tool and placed alongside the hole. That was repeated in the long trench for the electric wire, then a hole had to be dug for a septic tank. Add to that, the drainage lines, and then, of course we needed a fence. So you can see the exhausting steps of "simply digging holes." Yet, when the boys talk about those experiences at Trout Creek, they laugh. Well, not right away, they don't.

We soon had chickens, and kept them in a little fenced yard. We'd move the chickens to another area and then plant collard greens in the yard where they had been in. Yes! Awesome collard greens!! We had a small garden and soon we purchased a pig, who had the cleanest "pig pen" in town, made with a cement floor that could be washed off easily. We got a young calf, and named her Bambi. She was stubborn, rebellious and set in her ways from the time we brought her home. Then we purchased two horses. One was a large Morgan, we named "Blaze," a gelding, and the other, a cross between a Welch pony and Appaloosa horse, "Thunder." He was just plain mean. He kicked; he tried to throw us into barbed wire fences; he even had traits like a donkey: he would stop short, trying to throw us over his head. But it was a delightful mini-farm. The short time we lived there created memories we all hold dear. All of that was on a little half acre plot of clay.

We learned a visual lesson from Thunder. We had fenced the little "yard," and Dan decided it would be good if Thunder could eat the grass, and be some help to us! He tied Thunder to an old tire, thinking that as he grazed, he'd just naturally pull the tire around with him. That was a good plan, but Thunder didn't really comprehend "the whole picture." One day, he jerked the tire a little too hard and it twisted upright and began rolling. All Thunder could see was that tire, "coming after him as fast as it could!" His head turned back, enlarged eyes focused on the tire and his nostrils flared in fear as he went as fast as possible trying to get away from that tire. In doing so, he blasted through the bob wire fence and kept going as hard as his short legs could carry him . . . . with the tire right on his heels. Dan went after him and finally calmed in down and walked him home.

We learned a lot of lessons from that experience. That "seed" planted so deeply now, opened my spirit to see beyond Thunder and his fear. Many of us carry weights around, pounding on our heels as we try to outrun them. The faster we run, the more they pursue us. We need Someone to come along, quiet our spirits, and release us from those things that linger and cause us grief. We all need to be set free. If we let Jesus "loose" us, we can be free forever.

I left the police department when we married, and Dan left about a year and a half after we moved to Trout Creek. We were adjusting to "the cloud."

We suddenly had to find employment. We had purchased some investment property in another county, so we began our search there. We discovered a huge chicken farm—with a half million chickens at all stages of growth from baby chicks to the laying hens that were kept four to a cage. Dan began working with the brooder farm of about 60,000 chicks. That meant keeping the thousands of chicks from smothering themselves, keeping the "poop" cleaned up under them, and their huge building clean and disinfected. It also meant feeding, medicating, and "de-beaking" them. That's a story for another day.

After years as a clean cut Tampa police officer, this was quite a drastic change for Dan. His new routine was to begin the day facing those thousands of baby chicks, collect those who had smothered each other over night, feed and clean up after them, then come home at lunch and fall into the doorway. It was a huge adjustment to leave the comfort of a desk in a comfortable office, giving expert testimony in three courts, "lunching" with attorneys and judges, to shoveling chicken manure, coming home with feathers in his hair, and physically exhausted.

It wasn't very long until he was overseeing the seven "houses"—each with about 60,000 chickens at different phases of growth. One unit held 50,000+ growers, and the rest were laying hens. It was a tremendous responsibility, but the farm gave us a lovely home and Dan had a Jeep for his use around the farm. Our power bill was included in the package as well as pasture for our horses. The farm covered 300 acres. Dan's advancement caused some hard feelings among the other workers. He was new and a leas one other man had expected that promotion.

That one man stayed angry. One day, he just spit right in Dan's face. "You know, John," Dan said, the saliva dripping from his cheek, "I'm a Christian, and you should be very glad, because before I became a Christian, I would have put you down good." That was the end of that. But it was the second time he had faced that challenge. The first time, it happened right in the police station and it was another police officer who spit in his face. He answered him the same way.

These were hard lessons as a new believer, but Dan passed every one. He was putting into practice the Word he had planted deep in his heart.

We couldn't bring our growing calf, Bambi, to the chicken farm but the boys enjoyed riding the horses through the fields and back roads. Bambi was, probably because we tried to make a pet of her, extremely spoiled and rebellious. One time, Dan decided he was going to "break her stubborn streak," and tied her to the car and pulled. And pulled. Bambi resisted like we would if someone was demanding we do something we just *didn't want to do*. Bambi left deep ruts in the road as she resisted with all her might. She never did "lead."

Rebellion is compared to witchcraft in the Bible. Yes, it is! There are lots of ways to rebel against God. "Doing our own thing" is the definition of sin. Doing what pleases us, instead of pleasing the Lord our God. Rebellion is just that: insisting on having our own way instead of yielding to the loving hand of our Father.

CHAPTER SEVEN

Children—And Animals—Gifts and Lessons

When we left Trout Creek, I was pregnant. We had been married two years and had our hands full with my sons. Our income had been cut drastically after leaving the police department, and although the salary was low, the benefits on the farm were outstanding. There were the negatives, like billions of flies that came inside every time the door was opened, the smell of chicken manure when it was rainy, damp and humid. And then of course, there was the continual burning of the dead chickens. But life was good—anyway. All the eggs we could eat, and all the roosters we could catch and cook. [Roosters had no place on that egg laying farm.]

By the time our little son was born, we moved into the three bedroom, two bath home that was included with the promotion. A large picture window gave a beautiful view of the horses grazing or the boys racing home after a ride. Dan built a "hitching post" not far from the back door and it was a refreshing and delightful scene to see the boys ride up and tie them off. Dan and I rode through the woods and loved every minute of it. I rode right up to the time our son was born. It was during that time, we were racing through the pine forest when the other horses and riders curved to the left and so did the horse I was riding. I, however, kept going forward. Yes! It hurts when you fall. But I wouldn't have missed those years for anything in the world. A part of passion is the joy it brings (even with the pain!).

When David was old enough, he went to work picking eggs, not an easy job. It mean pushing a cart the length of a football field on an upward incline for half the walk, and downward on the second half. On both sides, he would pick up the eggs that had rolled out from under cages holding four hens each—packed closely together. There were about 50,000 laying hens producing as hard as they possibly could, and forced by a lighting technique to lay more than natural. The load became very heavy as the total increased, but he learned to work hard and save his money. The poor hens gave their all. After producing the high volume of eggs, then they were sold for soup or some such commodity. And, of course, the manure was sold as well. They gave their all . . . .

David was also getting to know other kids who lived and worked on the farm. Some of those relationships were not good. He eventually left home. There was no fight, no argument, nothing to point to a "reason"—he just didn't come home from school one day. That was a crushing experience and much of that time period I have blurred from my memory. I remember Dan told me I couldn't build a wall high enough if the children didn't want to stay there. It hurt to think they didn't. It was heartbreaking. David came back for a short time but left again.

While Craig and David were riding horseback through the woods, fishing in the ponds and shooting rabbits, the older boy was getting into trouble in another state. Police called to ask if he could come and live with us. I felt like he would be a bad influence on the other boys, but Dan encouraged me to be more forgiving, to give him every chance. We did and it wasn't long after he came to live with us that he left and took David with him.

When I discovered they were gone, I ran through the woods crying and screaming for them. I learned later that they hid and watched, laughing at me. That deep seated passion binds the broken heart and covers the hurt. David never returned to live with us again. It was difficult to understand how such a quiet, sweet, gentle young man could *just leave*. No discussion, no *reason*. The "reason" was probably right in my face, but I didn't . . . or refused to . . . see it. Craig was a natural horseman who needed no saddle, and would climb over Blaze's head to his back and ride off. He was as comfortable there as he would be riding a bike. Maybe more so. We continued to keep Thunder—as mean as he was—and nothing about him changed. But both Craig and David rode him with no problem.

Dan discovered a beautiful Tennessee Walker stallion penned in a very small enclosure on one of the back roads. It was love at first sight. He went by there as often as possible to make friends with him. *There was no gate to let him out of the tiny pen.* When Dan finally met the owner, he asked about that. "He's just too mean!" he snapped.

"How much do you want for him?" Dan asked.

"Oh, you won't be able to handle him. He's full of fire, mean as can be!" the old man scowled.

"Well, if I can get him to let me lead him, would you sell him to me?"

"That's not going to happen!" the guy was sure.

"You sure won't be able to handle him if there's a mare anywhere near!" he added.

Dan spent time talking to the horse, giving him snacks, and just plain "making friends" with him. The day finally came t hat Dan felt like he would be able to lead him home. By then, he had actually put a bit in his mouth and let him feel the reins against his neck. He took down one side of the pen and the stallion immediately reared up, but when Dan spoke gently to him, he stared at him and, slowly, hesitantly, yielded to the reins. Dan walked him home. That was the beginning of a love affair between the two. We named him "Red Feather." The horse loved him so much, he would do anything Dan asked of him. Sometimes, Dan would just hang the bit and reins over the hitching post and Red Feather would go over and nuzzle under the reins, as though trying to put them on himself. Dan taught him how to be still when he rode through the woods and shoot a rifle from his back. He liked to shoot cans, etc. so it wasn't long before Red Feather would see the can or whatever first and just stop gently, for Dan to shoot. Love conquered the fear. The Scripture says, "Love covers a multitude of sins."

Blaze, the Morgan, loved to run home, like most horses. So there was no competition when he was involved. However, on one such ride, Dan was on Red Feather and Craig was on Blaze.

There was a large pond behind the house and when the two horses got to that place, Blaze took a curve to the right and Red Feather made a decision to just "jump over it." With one leap, Dan flew over his head and came down hard in the mud. Red Feather came crashing down on top of him and let out a deep "ugh!" on landing; Craig saw enough of it to race to the house as fast as he could.

"Mom, Red Feather fell on top of Dan in the lake," he screamed. My mind was a flurry of questions. What were they doing in the lake? How could something like that happen? Should I call an ambulance or . . . . What!?

I heard hoof beats and laughter. "You should have seen Red Feather when he fell on me! No! You should have *heard* him! I don't know who was more surprised, him or me!" Dan laughed. Covered with mud, both Dan and Red Feather needed only a bath to restore them. Dan explained that as soon as Red Feather stood up, he had climbed on his back and nudged him toward home. Neither was the worse for it. But they didn't return that way any more.

We raised peanuts, potatoes, collard greens, and more corn than found in those famous "Ooooooklahoma" fields. In several areas of the farm there were mucky places where Dan planted acres of corn. It was "that high" as well, and much more than we could harvest or eat. So we offered it to the workers who lived on the farm. All they had to do was to pick it and eat all they wanted. But every one it was offered to commented that they'd take any we wanted to give them . . . . But they didn't want to pick it. So we harvested and shucked it and fed the horses. We learned a valuable lesson about people. It wasn't the last time we saw people respond that way.

CHAPTER EIGHT

God Knocks on the Door

There was a lot of activity in our spiritual lives. We learned how important it was to keep our eyes focused on Jesus—and no one else. We had several disappointments [read "We're Not All Cannibals!"] in our endeavor to follow Him. After many frustrations with "church," and "church people," *we agreed with some friends to open a church in our home!* Still doing a lot of horseback riding, we road through the woods and met many people who had moved away from the city thinking they could hide from God. Not! *We found 'em.* Many came to the church in the house. In fact, we have friends almost 40 years later, from that *church in the house.*

The Church grew until there were over eighty people meeting in our house—Sunday school classes in all the rooms [including bedrooms and kitchen]. We had four services on Sunday and one during the week with choir practice on the same night. There was an excitement as people found Jesus and began to follow Him. Dan led the singing and a friend began preaching, after some trepidation. He resisted God until everyone in the Church knew God was dealing with him (the most miserable person in the world is a believer running from God—or His calling). Everything seemed to be running smoothly . . . . Until . . . . God arrive don the scene.

The group purchased ten acres on a main street and began plans to build a sanctuary. On the day the foundation was being poured, Dan planned to be there to help "skreet" [level, I guess] the concrete.

That day he was working at the feed mill—grinding up chicken feed for the half million chickens. The mill was several miles from the farm, and also from the church property. While working at the mill, he also drove the feed truck and delivered the feed to the farm. He had to keep the machinery running and repair any breakdowns. Everything was automatic, but he had to oversee the mix and during the time he sat there, he punched buttons and kept his Bible open, grabbing a few verses here and there.

"Lord, You know I want to help the other men with the foundation," Dan prayed as he divided the mixture. "Lord, You're going to have to work it out for me to finish here in time to go over to the Church," he reminded Him.

Suddenly, he felt his body begin to "tremble." As he was praying, syllables began to flow from his lips that were unintelligible. His body kept shaking. I was working a few miles away and he called me.

"Geri, something is happening to me," he said. I could hardly understand him.

"*What's* happening?" I asked.

"I don't know. I just can't seem to stop my body from shaking," he said in gasps.

"There's something else," he added. "Some words are coming that I don't understand."

"Oh, Dan, you're just tired," I explained [as if I knew what was happening.]

"Why don't you call the pastor?" I asked, thinking that if it were a spiritual thing, the pastor would have the answer.

Well, Dan tried calling him but got no answer. We're pretty sure God's hand was in that, too, because later we learned the pastor would negate everything Dan was experiencing.

I don't remember much of that day, other than he got off in time to help with the foundation and we didn't speak much of the incident for a long while. Some things changed, however. Dan was . . . *different*. Remember, he always took the Word of God seriously and believed what it said *radically*. But from that time on, he had an outpouring of love that enveloped him and all around him. His background included a period when he was an apprentice mortician. As such, he had embalmed over a thousand bodies. He had driven an ambulance (long before there were "paramedics") and answered many accident scenes. He experienced more horror than any nineteen year old should encounter. When he became old enough, he joined the police academy and became one of Tampa's finest, a Tampa Police officer. He was exposed to more ghastly scenes and nightmares. Through all of this, his heart had been hardened because of the dreadfulness he was forced to deal with over the years. But now the Lord had taken that heart of stone that he used to protect himself, and gave him a soft heart of flesh.

He saw Scriptures that *I had never discovered before*. [And after all, I taught Sunday school for a long, long time!] He began believing for supernatural things like healing. Well, in our Church, we just concluded all our prayers with, "If it be Thy will." [We spoke King James English, like the apostle Paul.] We didn't really know much about the when, where and why God healed, so we covered it all with that little phrase.

Life on the chicken farm was busy. Dan's responsibilities increased. One day, Dan heard a loud banging coming from inside a large storage tower. The huge silos held tons of feed. He heard a muffled cry. Then he realized that one of the men had climbed up to check the level of feed and had fallen into the bin. In addition to the grain, there was the thick dust which would do irreparable damage to his lungs if he didn't get him out right away. He was down deep in the bin and Dan didn't know how to get him out.

"Dan! Pray! You know how to pray!" the words were barely audible. Dan knew he had to do something right away if his friend was going to live. He got a torch and burned a hole in the bin. That is not the safest thing to do, but it was what he felt *needed to be done*. And Old John lived to tell the tale.

"See what that kind of praying will do?" he asked Dan later. [Romans 8:26] It was *that kind of prayer* that broke through many barriers.

Life went on until one day I had a message from my friend in Melbourne, on the other side of the state.

"Geri, come over here," she pleaded. "Something is happening in my sister's Church that I don't understand. It has something to do with the Holy Spirit. Tell me everything you know about the Holy Spirit."

Not a big deal. After all, I *had been teaching Sunday school for many years.* But when I began to answer her, I realized my knowledge of the Holy Spirit was very limited. I knew there was a real "presence" sometimes when the invitational song was sung (Usually during several verses of 'Just as I am'). I knew that when an evangelist came to preach a revival, the Holy Spirit convicted people of their need to be saved. I remembered the "Doxology" we sang, "Praise God from Whom all blessings flow", ending with "Praise Father, Son and Holy Ghost. Amen." But beyond that . . . . nothing. So I began searching the Scriptures. There were a lot of verses about the Holy Spirit in both the old and new testaments. I was surprised.

My friend had given me a book, 'Like a Mighty Wind,' written by an Indonesian man named Mel Tari. He and his church had experienced a visitation of the Spirit of God exactly as the day of Pentecost in Acts the second chapter. I mean, it was *exactly like Acts 2—literal fire so real that the fire department was called.* People began speaking in languages they had never learned. Mel Tari understood some of the languages, because he had studied them, and he knew *the people speaking them did not understand what they were saying.* Interestingly, they were praising God in these new languages.

A second manifestation that was so very obvious was their joy. Immediately, they wanted to go and tell others about Jesus, His love and His salvation. Right away, they left two by two to visit other villages to share the good news about Jesus. As they walked, God continually manifested Himself by showing them miracles. They told everyone about the love of Jesus and the joy that had found in meeting Him in this new experience.

But that was Indonesia. On the other side of the world, as far as I was concerned. And I didn't really believe God did anything outside my own denomination. Besides, *this was a Presbyterian Church!* They had been fasting and praying for revival, meeting in the Church night after night. Then they had this awesome visitation from the Holy Spirit. They sought Him and He met them. [Jer. 29:13]

Dan came home for lunch and I told him about the book. *"That's just a book,"* he commented. "But these things are happening to these people!" I tried to explain. "Won't you just read a little bit of it?" I pleaded.

I think he might have glanced at it. But by then, I explained what was going on at Jane's and asked if he could take me over. When he quickly said, "Okay," again I felt that little "rush" that God had something up His sleeve. He surely did.

Dan drove me over to the west coast . . . *and left me there* with the understanding that Jane would bring me home the next week.

That was a Divine Appointment if I've ever had one. But no, I hadn't. Jane's husband was out of town and I was there without my husband, so we acted like the schoolgirls we were down deep. We went to the Christian book store and got an armload of books about the Holy Spirit. While we were there, we picked up an invitation to a "Full Gospel Business Men's Fellowship." We giggled about that, saying we should go since were "on our own." The clerk explained it was for men *and* women, but we disregarded it.

We went back to Jane's and sat on the floor with the books scattered around our feet. We were grabbing a thought here and a phrase there.

"Look what this says," Jane grabbed me.

"Yeah, but listen to this!" I recounted.

On we went. We were still going over the books when Jane's husband surprised us by coming home early.

"Do you girls want to go to a dinner tonight up in Cocoa Beach?" he asked.

"Sure! Where?" we both blurted out.

"It's called a "Full Gospel Business Men's Fellowship" dinner, he answered. A chill went up my back as Jane and I both quickly looked at each other.

Then, of course, we giggled.

"Sure!" we answered.

CHAPTER NINE

"I'll Never Be the Same Again, Oh, No!"

It was a cold January night as we drove north along the ocean highway to Cocoa Beach. I watched as the waves crashed against the shore; it looked so bitter out there! But it was a night I would remember for the rest of my life.

We arrived at the hotel among people greeting each other with laughs and hugs. It was certainly a happy group! The dining room was lovely and the food delicious. Then the program began! First there was singing—no! I can't call it "singing." It was worship as I never experienced "worship." There was an emotion coming from the group that was hard to identify. It seemed to be *truly worship*. I've been to church all my life, but all of a sudden I was in the midst of *worship*. I was touched deeply in my spirit. There were a few announcements of upcoming activities and the speaker was introduced. He was a young teacher, who shared his testimony. In all my years of "church attendance," I had never ever heard anything like it.

He had been an agnostic—who claimed not to believe in *anything or anybody*—and taught high school "drop outs," who were given a last chance in his class. He was totally frustrated. He went home and decided to commit suicide. He purchased a gun, some liquor, drank it, and put the barrel to his temple. Suddenly, he heard a voice in his spirit say, "If you shoot yourself, you'll go to hell. If you're going there, don't you think you should learn something about it?"

He was shocked and a little drunk. He wondered how he would "find out about hell." He searched his apartment, stumbling from chair to couch to the bookcase, where he found a dusty old Bible. He didn't even remember it being there. As an English teacher he naturally began reading at the very beginning of the book. Every evening after work, he would come home, exhausted and frustrated, open a bottle of liquor, put his feel up and read the Bible. He read and read—all the way through the Old Testament. Then he began the New Testament. When he read the third chapter of the book of John, something stirred inside him. Tears suddenly streamed down his face. What was happening to him? He read, "For God so loved the world . . ." Suddenly, he knew "the world," included him! In his innermost being, he knew beyond a shadow of a doubt that *God sent Jesus to die for him*. God loved him that much! It took his breath away. He continued to read.

By the time he completed his testimony—with experiences I had never in my whole life heard of—the baptism in the Holy Spirit—Deliverance from evil spirits—powerful ministry to the street kids—I began to sob. I wiped the tears with my lovely linen napkin and cried some more. Suddenly I felt my arms lift up above my head—but I knew my arms were hanging by my side! I lifted my head with my eyes closed—and saw a bright light shining down on me. I felt myself being lifted up above the floor. But I knew my feet were firmly planted. So much was happening, I hardly heard the man when he called me forward—only a couple of steps because we were sitting right in front of the speaker's table. Others came to pray for me. I hadn't asked for prayer. Someone said, "You're asking for a miracle, aren't you?" Well, the "happenings" around me were more than I could handle at that point. But I said, "Sure, I guess so." Might as well get all I could get at that point, I thought. They prayed, I went back to my seat and after some chit-chat, we returned to Jane's house.

All the way back, there was chatter about the music, the food, the "did you see . . . . ?" Finally Jane's husband said, "What actually happened to you, Geri? We all know *something was happening. What was it??*"

I didn't want to do anything to eliminate the aura that had surrounded me. I pretty much dismissed him and basked in the sweet Spirit I had never before encountered. Jane took me home and promised to come back the next weekend to attend a Charismatic Conference in Tampa. She didn't make it, but Dan and I went. At the end of many messages from men with various anointings, several "invitations" were given: for salvation, for healing, for deliverance, for the Baptism in the Holy Spirit, for those who had received the Baptism in the Holy Spirit but had not spoken in tongues . . . . At that point, Dan nudged me and said, "That's for you. *Get in that line.*" I did.

"Have you received the Baptism in the Holy Spirit?" the young man asked as I approached him. Wow! I thought. That must have been what happened to me last weekend! But no one said anything about speaking in tongues. He waited for my answer.

"Yes! Yes, I did! Last weekend!" I stammered. Then, as I heard my own words, I realized *that was exactly what had happened to me.*

"Well, you can pray in your personal prayer language any time you want to!" the young man explained simply.

I opened my mouth to do just that, and words began to flow with a language. I had never learned. There were no bells and whistles—I had all those the week before. Instead, there was a quiet assurance and peace that God was speaking—using my vocal chords and my voice. Wow! This was the beginning of an unbelievable adventure into an unfamiliar spiritual realm of supernatural passion.

The first immediate manifestation—and I usually explain it to everyone I minister to—is that voice inside my head began to taunt, "That's just you making up those sounds!" or "That doesn't sound like anyone else when they speak in tongues! It must not be real!"

As if there were an angel on one shoulder and a devil on the other, I heard another voice: "You received this gift from God and, and every gift from God is good. If it weren't real, the enemy wouldn't work so hard to make you doubt and stop praying. So right then and there, I made a commitment to pray in tongues every single day of my life—just to show the devil how real it was! And so many years later, I still do.

Chapter Ten

God's Plans Never Cease to Amaze Us

My friend had been healed at a Kathryn Kuhlman meeting many years before, so when she held one of her last healing meetings in Tampa, we decided to go. We knew a man who was confined to a wheel chair and we were sure if we fasted and prayed, God will heal him completely. We fasted and took him to the meeting. We were able to get him in because of the wheelchair, but we had to stand in line *for many hours*. It was worth it just for the worship. Dino, the pianist, was anointed and the anointing fell on the audience. As we worshipped, Ms. Kuhlman would point a long slender finger and announce, "You! Diabetes! You're healed!" Stand up! Polio, you're healed! Stretch your legs!" She kept calling out healings that were taking place and it kept getting later and later. Our friend finally left without his healing. We are confused. ***What did WE do wrong?***

After fasting all week, we looked for anything that was open so we could grab a bit to eat on the way out of town. We stopped at a McDonald's on the bank of the Hillsborough River in Sulphur Springs, in north Tampa. It was late, but we chose to sit outside on the picnic benches. There was a couple at one table and a man sitting alone at another.

We brought our food to the table and prayed over it.

"What did you have to do that for?" the lone man yelled at us from his table.

"What did we do?" we asked.

"You know what you did, praying like that!" he growled.

Well, there we were, my friend and I, my son and his girlfriend. We prayed quietly, and definitely not "in his face."

The couple got up and left.

He walked over to our table. We prayed harder and quieter.

He addressed me, "Why did you do it?" he asked.

"We always pray over our meals," I answered.

"But you don't know what's going on," he said. His voice was a little quieter, even a little sad.

Then he told us his story.

"My beautiful wife was a missionary. She loved the Lord." He caught his breath. It was obvious he had been drinking. And God took her away from me!" A tear rolled down his cheek as he sobbed.

"What happened?" I asked.

"She had cancer. She was diagnosed and in no time, she was gone. Just like that!" he said, shaking his head in disbelief as more tears streamed down his face. "That's why I've come here tonight." With that remark, he showed us the bag he had been concealing. His decision was to sit there in the darkened part of the picnic area and drink until he had the nerve to shoot himself.

"You loved her and you know she loved the Lord," I began. "You also know that she is with Jesus in Heaven," I continued. "Don't you think she would be terribly hurt to know that you have decided to do such a terrible thing?" My eyes pleaded with him silently. "I think that would break her heart!"

At that, he broke down in convulsive sobs. "I know that! I know that!" he repeated. "But it hurts so bad to lose her! I can't live without her!"

I knew everyone at the table was praying. The Lord didn't let us rush or be fearful. It was obvious now why He had called us to fast. His ideas are always better than ours.

"What do you think God wants you to do?" I asked. "Have you ever asked Jesus to come into your heart and be your Savior?"

"Yes, I have. But I got mad and turned away when He took my bride." He sobbed.

"Well, *you know God hasn't stopped loving you!* He wants you to come back to Him. In fact, He sent us here at this very time and lace to tell you that very thing!" I explained—and realized the truth of what I was saying even as the words were spoken.

"Do you really believe that?" he asked—some hope was now showing in his countenance.

"Of course. What's your name?" I asked.

"Jack. Jack Shepherd," he answered.

"Well, Jack, why don't we make things right with Jesus and let Him show you how very much He loves you!"

"Okay," he said quietly, his head lowered. "What do I need to do?"

At that point we prayed with Him, asking Jesus to forgive him for turning away, for being angry at Him, and for considering suicide. He repeated the words after us.

"Oh!" he said. "Something happened!" With those words, he quickly went to his car and grabbed bottles of liquor. He poured the liquor on the ground. Then he took the empty bottles and tossed them in the trash container. He went back to the car and brought out a gun. We held our breath. He walked down the bank to the river and we heard the splash as he tossed the pistol into the water. We looked at each other. What an experience!

When he came back, he sat down, relaxed and at peace. We got some information from him so we could keep in touch. For a long time afterward, we sent him helps, and encouragement. He responded and we knew the Lord had put someone else in his life to continue to be there for him. Oh, God, You are sooooo good!

Since we don't always know God's whole plan, it's important to *"just mind."* That's what passion does: it walks by faith, sometimes now knowing "the whole story."

CHAPTER ELEVEN

POWER STRUGGLE

There are times in a passionate relationship that the passion itself gets tested severely. It surely happened to us. Learning to be a wife, yielding to another man fathering my children, and caring for both a toddler and teenagers, tested us to the limit. I had been a Christian most of my life and now *my husband thought he knew something!* Every subject seemed to cause resistance from one of us. [Usually me!] The struggle continued and my feelings were forever getting hurt. But it didn't stop me from all the rebellion I could muster.

Most Sunday mornings there was some kind of trauma. At this time, Dan was leading worship and the choir at our Church. I'd go to Church with my eyes red from crying and Dan was adored by all . . . . I took offense easily and often. There was a period of time when we hardly spoke for months. All that time, we were going to church, doing our "thang," and acting the role. Yes, I know what the word is. We finally decided we'd better "get over it" if we were going to "live the Christian life." Dan frequently told that we were always committed to the marriage, but not always committed to each other. The "D" word was not allowed in our vocabulary. Often, that just meant we didn't speak.

Soon after we received the Baptism in the Holy Spirit, He [the Holy Spirit] began a severe house cleaning of our spirits. He'll do that, you know. Dan's life experiences had hardened his heart. As a police officer, he was faced with new and unimaginable horrors. He was called to the scene in the police locker room shortly after going on duty one day. There, he found a jail guard shot and killed as he and an officer were playing "fast draw." There were more serious scenes, of course, but none so up close and personal. We had both worked with that guard for many shifts.

I didn't understand Dan's background or his home life. His heart seemed tender toward me, but it was easy enough for him to cut himself off from me. I lashed out. I struggled against him. I resisted his efforts to make things right. I wanted "all the words." I wanted him to hold me and tell me everything was going to be all right. I wanted. I wanted. But those were not the days when I even tried to understand him. It was consistently "all about me." I see that so much these days. If only we could reach inside those who are hurting so and "make it all better." I've learned that prayer—*believing prayer*—is the best answer. God can fix any personality if we only let go of it and stop trying to be God.

We went to some Bible studies and I found myself being obnoxious (I know. You just can't believe that!) by quickly answering any questions before Dan ever had a chance. What was I trying to prove? Finally, I caught myself doing it and stopped. But not right away.

Rebellion is the absence of obedience. It's the opposite of that "four letter word," submission. It's compared to witchcraft in the Bible. [Yes, it is!] I can understand that. It's another part of "control." I surely understand control . . . . I learned that submission was *not having to have your own way.*

Dan was always faithful to his commitments. So we had a date every week. We'd go out, have dinner, maybe even see a movie, and never speak. Looking back, it was surely infantile and ridiculous. But most of "growing up" is. We struggle when just being quiet works best. I don't mean "not speaking," but just being quiet enough to *listen to the other person.* I was so rebellious that if Dan asked me to do a little chore when he left for work, I'd make sure it was the very last thing I'd do before he came home. Why? Who knows? ***Attitude!!! Bad!***

Dan felt the Lord was calling him to be a pastor. He talked to our pastor about it but his response was that he didn't "witness" to it. It was discouraging to Dan, because he felt he had somehow missed God. But the Lord kept nudging, and one day another pastor *did* witness to the call on his life and offered to ordain him. So one Sunday in that small church, Dan was set apart as a pastor. The very next day, at his job as maintenance supervisor at a large condominium, he was in the elevator when an older woman stepped in and said to him, 'You're a minister, aren't you?" That "whoosh" of God's Spirit flowed over Dan as though He were adding His own "setting apart" for that call. Dan replied with a smile, "Yes Ma'am, I am."

CHAPTER TWELVE

ON THE SIDELINES

My oldest son, Jay, has lived a life of turmoil—finally settling in Texas. He had difficulties in relationships and a roller-coaster life living, as his brother said, "always on the edge." He's faced many traumas in his spirit and in his body. God healed him to testicular cancer, saved his leg that was damaged severely when he was a teenager, and lost the love of his life through suicide.

Working through a twelve step program, he asked me to visit him at his home. I went for a week and helped him work through his relationship with me and all the problems he felt I had caused him. I'm sure that much of his life's hurts were caused by the divorce from his father, and situations caused by that experience. He was thrown into a lifestyle that was a negative turning point for him and it was hard for him to get back on track. I take responsibility for much of it, but in the end, there comes a time when we have to face our choices and decisions and deal with them. Sometimes I feel I just need (and I'm probably right) to stay in an attitude of repentance for all the bad choices I've made over the years and how they have affected people—especially those closest to me. At the end of that week, I was physically and emotionally exhausted. Dan met me at the plane and took me to my favorite Mexican Restaurant. I sat down and all I could do was sob. And sob some more. It was a breaking point for me.

David had not contacted us for a long time after he left home. One Saturday, I was in Tampa with a friend visiting a half-way house, sharing communion with them. Several interesting things happened. The pastor used the Scripture that says, "Unless you eat My body and drink My blood, you are no part with Me." I had **NEVER** heard that verse used. That was ***powerful!*** Then, he asked if anyone had unforgiveness toward any of the other boys in the house. One by one, they would confess, "I'm sorry I skipped out on doing the dishes last night," or "I was late coming in. Forgive me, please," or "I didn't do the laundry on time this morning. I'm sorry. I'll do it right away." "Forgive me for swearing at you." That went on for quite a while, and I wondered what the average Church would do if faced with that kind of challenge before communion.

As we left, one of the young men asked if we needed prayer. I thought about David. "I haven't heard from my son for a long time. I have reason to believe he's involved with drugs. Will you pray for him please?"

"Sure, we'll send out 'Supplication' and 'grace,' the guy answered confidently.

My friend and I looked at each other with obvious questions.

"They're just angels. It's in the Bible," he explained. "They'll fine him."

I didn't think any more about it, but four days later, in the middle of the night, there was a knock on the door. It was David.

"Mom, some friends and I have been to Orlando to get some drugs. I've shot everything imaginable into my arms, hands and even feet and I can not get a high from anything," he explained. "The most unusual thing is, that everywhere I went someone told me, 'Jesus loves you.' I give up."

I heard Dan walking softly down the hall and return to the bedroom. I knew he was praying. Before sunrise, David had prayed, been baptized in the Holy Spirit, and delivered from the addiction to drugs. He fell asleep praying in the Spirit.

I hated to see him leave to go back home to Tampa. But later, I learned that he met the woman he later married the very next day, and they joined the military together. Today, many years later, I am enjoying their children and grandchildren. My great grandchildren are now in their teens and I stand amazed at a God who would make it possible for me to live long enough to enjoy them as my husband, a pastor, baptized them. More about that later.

Craig graduated from high school and surprised us by announcing he had [already] joined the military. He and I had been friends and I missed his humor and the fun we had together. Soon after he arrived in Anchorage Alaska, at Elmendorf AFB, he met a young woman and married. Some time later, he called to say they were expecting a baby and wanted us to come for the birth. We had no idea we could possibly afford a trip to Alaska, but our son, Chip, began to "confess" to *everyone who would listen that, "WE ARE GOING TO ALASKA."*

Dan told me to reserve our tickets on the airline and if the money "didn't show up," we would cancel. Otherwise, we'd be ready. The plan was for me to go two weeks earlier than Dan and Chip. Days went by and there didn't seem to be any possibility of our getting enough money together for the tickets. Of course we would not "charge" it or "use the card." If the cash wasn't there, we wouldn't make the trip.

Dan kept telling me to be ready, "just in case." Instead, I was more and more frustrated. One day, I prayed, "Lord, if we are going to be able to make that trip to Alaska, let me hear it from Dan's mouth *today.*" Yes, it *did* sound a little demanding.

When Dan arrived home that afternoon from work, his first words were, "We're going to Alaska!" I was shocked and thrilled.

We had a sailing sloop moored near his work and a man had asked him if he would sell it. He offered Dan within $20 of the cost of the airline tickets, and the rest, as they say, is history. We went to Alaska.

I was there with my son for some mother/son time, which was excellent. The first thing he wanted me to do was to make some "crab shoulau" and he brought home fresh Alaskan King Crab (what else?) to cook. I was there for the birth of my granddaughter, Joy, which was awesome. And supernatural. Read about in it "Count it all Joy" [published in 2000 by AuthorHouse].

Dan and I had a renewed passion when we saw each other after two weeks apart. Remember the movies? Those scenes when the lovers clutched each other hungrily? Luscious!

We enjoyed the dry cold and watched the snow drift down the mountains as the days darkened and the temperature dropped. We picked blueberries high in the mountains and Dan and the boys fished for trout and salmon. We ate smoked salmon prepared by a military friend next door on the base and spent the first few days of little Joyo's life with her. It was a shock to arrive at the Tampa Airport and step into the humid, steamy Florida weather. It nearly took our breath away. It was a different world. But how we praised God for the adventure of a lifetime.

It was He who made it happen, and it was our passion for Him that made it such a rush that the thrill lingers even today, so many years later. Passion opens the door to adventure and saturates the desire for such excitement.

CHAPTER THIRTEEN

THE PASSION OF FRIENDSHIP

Over the years I have been blessed with a multitude of true friends. On reflection, I realize how unique and unusual that is. So many years! So many friends! So many circumstances! I've had friends that I ran to in times of trouble. Others were right there to run *for me* to solve a problem or find one little detail.

The Bible talks about a friend who is closer than a brother [Prv 18:24b] and one who is willing to lay down his life for his friend. I know Jesus is the ultimate friend and the One who certainly laid down his life for us. But when I was a young mother, I was distressed about everything, and everyone. Every situation seemed devastatingly hopeless. One day I shared my desperation with my neighbor, who lived across the street. I was in such despair I was thinking seriously of ending my life. I wasn't making any sense, and she stayed with me all day—gave of herself completely to walk me through that period until I "came to my senses." [II Tim. 2:26]

It was that same friend who dropped everything, when she lived hours and miles away, and came to my call for help when my husband left me. She drove the several hours to reach my home and took care of my children until I could find more permanent help. She gave up her life for mine more than once!

When we lived on Minnow Creek, we had a good sized inboard-outboard boat. It pulled water skis and the kids loved it. We pulled Craig out in the Atlantic (later realizing how very, very deep the water was!) through the Sebastian Inlet to the Indian River, caught fish and cooked them on the bank. We pulled Jay on Christmas Day around a large lake and "made the day" for him. We took leisurely trips down the Hillsborough River and into the Tampa channel where the huge commercial ships docked. One of my sweetest memories is that we took some "movies (8 mm of course) of my parents and Chip riding the Geri G through the Hillsborough River, with all the scenes along the way. We took friends for moonlight boat rides, having picnics as we watched the sun go down. That was a favorite thing for us to do, as well.

But the "Geri G" often broke down. There are many stories that go along with the water adventures of that boat. One fourth of July, we took the boat out and when we docked, I took one of those steps you only see in the movies: when I stepped from the boat to the dock, my legs split and I went down. It would have been a funny scene, except that my foot fell on an oyster shell, which sliced it open from side to side. My knight in shining armor grabbed me and carried me up the bank to the house and pulled the two sides together with a bandage. It was a

Saturday, plus the holiday (if you're asking why we didn't go to the ER). We expected it to heal fairly quickly, because I was careful to stay off it. But it didn't. Instead, it became very painful. Extremely painful.

After a few days, we went to the doctor and a sliver of shell was seen when the foot was x-rayed. He took it out (Yeowww!) and all the other stuff that goes along with it and told me to definitely stay off it.

I was stuck in bed with a family to feed, laundry to do, all that goes with being the mother of the house. God chose to give me a visual of the body of Christ. (He told me later that's what He was doing.) The lady across the creek came over and changed my bed and washed my hair!!!!! Someone else came and cleaned house. Another someone did the laundry. There were meals brought in and loving gestures from people I hardly knew. God was expressing His love through each of them. How totally cool is that?!

My dear friend had a devastating divorce and asked to come and stay with us. There was no room at all, but she just wanted to be near us. What she didn't tell us was that she was addicted to Valium. One day she decided she'd "kick the habit" cold turkey. That is, stop taking it all at once. She passed out and seemed to have a heart attack. I remember praying like crazy for her to live and not die. She lived. But not long afterward, Dan heard a "thump" in the bathroom, and we had to break through, where we found her unconscious on the floor. We called 911 and she was hospitalized. This is a woman who gave and gave and gave to my family in every way. As a guest, she was perfect. She was encouraging, helpful and there was never any dissention at all. She stayed for over a year, in a very small area of the house that had previously been used as an office when I wrote for a local newspaper—using an old IBM typewriter at that!

But she was very beautiful, and my husband was a young pastor. There was gossipy chattering going on among our church folks. I told her she'd have to find a place of her own. That broke her heart, and mine as well. This is a woman who would never do anything to hurt us, or the Church we pastored. This is a friend who would go out of her way to do things to help and encourage us. This decision hurt our friendship temporarily, but the passion of friendships are never damaged permanently.

A few years later, through some strange misunderstanding, with no explanation whatsoever, she broke off our relationship. She was adamant about not wanting to continue our friendship in any way, shape or form. I was crushed, and only someone who has *friends* understands what an emptiness the loss of a friend brings. It's unlike any other bond. What made that worse, is that I never knew what I did to offend her. It was over a year of silence that ended only with a call to "Let's have lunch." When I asked about clearing the air, she declined, saying it was in the past and she wanted to leave it there. It hurt. But love forgives and forgives. Love does not take offense, and it doesn't keep a record of wrongs done to it. [I Cor 13]

Again, the seed of passion that originated in Jesus, lived in us both and caused us to maintain our friendship until her death. In fact, she waited for me to be with her before she went to be with Jesus. We were friends for over twenty five years.

I don't even remember how I met Alicia. A tiny little woman, she seemed to be one who was always there. We took Chip to Christian School, which was about 50 miles away , and often she would pick him up and bring him home. She was there for so many things—so helpful in big and small ways. She had stressors that kept attacking her and she came to us often. But the seed. The seed was kept alive through the years and recently we've been especially close. Another 30+ year friendship because of "the seed."

We had a home fellowship for many years and while we lived on Minnow Creek, we were in a cramped situation that absolutely no one [but me] noticed. Sitting on the floor, squeezed onto couches and chairs, we formed friendships that are still strong. One night, there was a disturbance outside the door. Some friends decided to bring another couple with them. The wife of the "other couple" was quite resistant to the idea, but they "drug her in," kicking and screaming. I tell the story that way, because that's always been the way she has recalled it. She became a strong and committed part of our fellowship and became quite active in drama, music, mime and prison ministry. Later, she even traveled to Russia to share her love for Jesus. I just received a call from her—we, too, have stayed in touch for over 30 years—to encourage me because (by email) she knew I was facing some "issues" in my late life. Our friendship has grown stronger as the seed has blossomed and bore fruit in each of our lives. The love we have for each other has encouraged the gifts and graces the Lord has placed within us. How good He is!

Early in our Church history, a couple of retired teachers joined us. They were both Jewish believers and excellent Bible teachers. They had moved down from New York and we grabbed them immediately to glean some of their deep insight into the Word. The husband had a heart condition and they hadn't been with us very long before he went to be with the Lord. It was a dramatic experience (you didn't expect anything else, did you?) as Dan and I visited him in the hospital. He asked, "Dan, I need to know my sins are forgiven." Dan quoted the Word that gave us permission to forgive sin. "Yes, Jack, your sins are forgiven." He took a deep breath of peace and slipped away into the arms of the Lord. His widow moved soon afterward to California and for several years we didn't communicate. Then, when Dan passed away, a mutual friend contacted her and we've been in touch ever since.

Jane and I met when we both attended middle school. We lived close to each other, and went to the same Church. We walked to school together (yes, several miles) and talked all the way. We met after school and talked our way home. When we got home, one or the other of us would call and we'd talk until one of the parents demanded we "get off that phone!" I don't know what we talked about then, but we still love it.

Jane and I have spent hours, days and weeks at her mountain house, sitting on the swing on the long porch, listening to the mountain water rush over the rocks below. Sounds of the early morning included trucks climbing the steep road on the other side of the stream, the large tires crunching the rocks along the winding path. We climbed the side of the mountain behind the house and overlooked the view. We talked all the way up and back down again. We spent days shopping the flea markets, digging into the old favorites that some mountaineer passed along. And we talked.

Jane's house became my safe place because of our tender friendship. When Dan and I were experiencing the most stringent test of our relationship, I ran away. To Jane's house, of course. She and her family lived on the east coast of Florida and one day, I just called and told her I was in my car, headed her way. No questions. She just let me crawl in the guest room, where I stayed for about a week. She was an RN and went to work, checked on me, and left me alone. I knew she was praying for me and God worked out all the details. She has always been there for me, always a better friend to me than I was to her.

In early 2000, she called, inviting me on a trip to Israel, which was pretty impossible from my viewpoint. But I did get to go, took another friend with me as a room mate, and spent two whole weeks climbing in and out of tour buses, eating al the new and unique delicacies never tasted before, listening to more information than I could possibly assimilate, took more pictures than I knew what to do with when I returned, and spent luscious time on balconies overlooking the Mediterranean. The banquet style buffets at every meal were superb and the accommodations were so outrageous we actually checked at the desk in one hotel to make sure ours was the suite with the two balconies and Jacuzzi!

We prayed in the old Garden of Gethsemane among olive trees that had been there during Jesus' day. Old, gnarled and secure, the trees remained in tact throughout the years and bombardments on the old city. The tour guide allowed us in through a locked gate and suggested we find an area of our choosing in the garden and take time to pray. Of all the places we ventured, that surely was the one where I experienced God's Spirit and felt His presence the dearest. We walked the places He walked, we took communion together, went to the upper room and got there just as a group was singing Amazing Grace acapella. The music filled the room and the glory of the Lord saturated every space.

We visited some old digs, like Peter's mother in law's house. We spent time in the Old City of Jerusalem, walking along the stone path through the city—the Villa del a Rosa. We saw a mother with a small child sitting outside the city gate begging. We saw trash was being thrown in the area of the Eastern Gate, where we expect Jesus to stand some day. We prayed at the Western Wall and realized the faith being demonstrated in the thousands of prayer requests tucked into the crevices of the wall. We sat along the bank of the Galilee and imagined what it was like as the ground was covered by people hungry to hear Jesus teach. We chose to be water baptized in the Galilee instead of the Jordan because of the tourist activity at the Jordan. We understood why Jesus walked on the water. The bed of the Galilee was soooo rocky! We saw the hill called Golgotha and couldn't imagine the sacrifice that was demonstrated there two thousand years ago. We saw the empty tomb and rejoiced that we know our Savior lives on today as He did when he left that borrowed crypt.

But Jane had lost her husband not long before and was suffering most of the time in a grief I was unable to understand. I didn't know how to help her. I still don't understand the grief that comes with such loss. Everyone I know grieves differently.

Dan had such strong faith—especially for healing—and he would always go to Matthew 6:33 for directions as to what to do for any physical attack. He had been losing a lot of weight (a LOT of weight!) when one night he became very short of breath. *I have a friend* I called for prayer. She brought over a machine of some sort to produce oxygen to help him. I called Chip, who came down from his home about an hour away. The solution was very simple to him: take Dad to the hospital immediately. He was angry with me for not calling the paramedics. His dad pleaded to let him wait until the next day. I'm still not sure why. He suffered all night unable to breath except with the oxygen. The next morning we made the decision to call the paramedics to take him to the hospital, but when I called the doctor, he suggested we could drive him over since we were just a few minutes from the hospital. I explained that he couldn't breathe and the machine we were using wouldn't fit in the car. I was asked if I had a small tank. I called my friend. She did. She explained it wasn't full, so I called the doctor's office to explain. My friend brought the tank over, and we called the hospital to let them know we were on our way with a small tank and would need assistance as soon as we arrived.

I gave my friend the necessary paper work and she took care of that while I went with Dan into the ER area. Judy did everything possible for her pastor and friend. In a couple of days, the fluid was reduced (congestive heart failure) and he was able to come home. For the next four months, he was back to normal, fishing, boating, chopping down trees, spending time and lunches with his friends, and then the end came. Judy had made the comment that he would not have a lingering illness, eh would "just leave." That's exactly what he did. Judy was there again to do the necessary things. I never went to the funeral home. She made all the arrangements. She drove the long trip to my son's house to bring papers for me to sign, drove back and forth to save the heartbreak. She was that friend who was closer than a brother, who laid down her life for me. It will always be a time of gratitude, of sweet remembrance.

Another friend I met when she was going through her "ragamuffin" state. It was "in" to go to Church with holes in your jeans, stringy hair, and a general "unkempt" look. It was also during one of times I was learning to "accept people where they are." [Romans 15:7] I'm so glad I met her. That was twenty plus years ago and we've had a loving friendship that has grown as we have. She was in an abusive relationship, and once she escaped that, went on to be the manager in an office where I worked the one and only time as a switchboard operator. When she asked me to come to work for her, I was in a place in my life when I was desperate for "something" that would make me feel good about myself. It happened. Even though I had no experience, I was accepted and encouraged. Interestingly, I was the wife of a pastor of a Church and the Lord let me know right away to be quiet about "all that." I did, and had great relationships while working there. It was an hour drive through hills and beautiful countryside, with the view of a serene flock of sheep on the way.

Later, as she became successful in her field, she amazed me with the wisdom the Lord gave her. It wasn't always active in her persona life, but today, even though she has had some tumultuous experiences and moved far, far away, I thank the Lord that she is always there for me and our relationship has probably never been closer.

It's that seed again! Someone mentioned to me this week, *"EVERYTHING BEGINS WITH A SEED."* [Gal 5] *I knew that*, so why was it such a surprise to hear? We need to be reminded sometimes. Often, actually. This is a friend who has my attention when she calls me to accountability. I have allowed her to be that close and I accept it from her. I don't always like it, but I know it is honest and it is from her heart to mine.

I have another "old" friend, younger than me, but one whose life I've shared both near and far. She, too, has lived many years of trauma and distress. It seems that the more difficult the circumstances, the more gracious, loving, and kind she has become. I have always thought of her as a one of the most godly women I knew, but even she has had her share of dramatic temptations in the flesh. I've watched as her children have disappointed her, devastated her with their lifestyles and yet others have honored her with the godly choices they've made. She is very dear and I cherish her friendship.

I am so blessed, I could go on and on. Yesterday I got a call from another friend, one whose lifestyle has changed many times over the years, yet that precious seed has held us close. When I hear her voice, it is one that I love. We are surely sisters in the spirit. Another friend comes to mind, who has always been there to "bring me to myself"—to shock me with the truth and get my attention when my life wants to take a turn for the worse—that is, a turn to doing things "my way." How blessed I am that she loves me enough to tell me the truth and she always does.

There was one who just chose to "dismiss me." After over thirty years, going through a multitude of life and death experiences, she chose to close the door on our friendship. Just like that! Yes! Of course I did something that angered her. Yes! I've asked for forgiveness for my behavior. But it seemed there would never be reconciliation. Then a mutual friend passed away and I called to let her know. "I'm so glad you called," she said. "I've been wanting to talk to you." It was so refreshing to hear her voice with no "walls" between us. As you can tell, I do truly appreciate my friendships. They are a precious commodity in this world of trauma, hurt feelings and stress.

As my memory flashes pictures of these faces I've known over the years, I thank God for each of them, and thank Him for bringing them into my life . . . . *and keeping so many of them there over the years!*

Reviewing those who have touched my life in the most subtle ways, I think of the lady I met in the paint department at a local store. By the time we had made our selections, we had also exchanged names and addresses—and have been corresponding ever since!

Correspondence has been at the core of many friendships. The daughter of a friend got into serious trouble and went to prison. We began to write to each other and the Lord used me to encourage her, and she encouraged me as well. During her imprisonment, she lost her aunt, her mother, both grandparents and a son during the 14 year confinement. At her son's funeral, there were more young people than I had ever seen at a funeral for any age. I did my best to take photos of the surreal scene. It was the closest she could be and I know it was more than heartbreaking. But I did my best to help her "be there" to see how he was loved. Who knows why God puts certain people in our lives? It is a glorious plan.

I've just had a short hospital stay. While there, one of the nurses commented as I was being wheeled in, that she thought she knew me. Another one of those subtle touches. Years before, I had "met" her as the window teller at my bank, got acquainted, and then ran into her as she began working for a local food store. We exchanged pictures of our children and in my case, my grandchildren, and again, we exchanged addresses and I stayed in touch with her for a long time, then it ended. Now, years later, she told me her story, as I was being "loaded" onto the bed, crisp white sheets tucked neatly under me and pillows fluffed beneath my head. She was anxious to share what had happened since we'd been in touch. She related the accomplishments which included going back to school and taking the educational steps of medical success until she found herself now as the charge nurse in the cardiac care unit. I was quick to let her know how proud I was of her endeavors to improve herself and be a good provider as a single mother for her two children, now 16 and 20 years old. I don't remember ever seeing her so happy. How good the Lord is to bring those sweet friends and acquaintances into our path—how refreshing! What a joy!

When we first moved to Spring Hill, I met the owners of the Christian Book store—before most purchases were made on line. The shop was a ministry for them, and the two high school teachers took turns taking vacation time from school and running the store. I became close friends with them and they became very earnest prayer partners. They retired from teaching after twenty years, then operated the store for the next twenty. That friendship has been ongoing for over twenty five years and I cherish the ability to call on them for prayer at any time. We're connected more by Email now than phone, but that has become a very personal genre of communication.

Today I received a letter from yet another long time friend. In fact, you might remember I mentioned them a few chapters ago. He was tall and blond, she a tiny dark haired girl. They loved the Lord and had children. They seemed to be the perfect family. Over the years we have run into each other, visited off and on, and corresponded in these last few years. What a joy to have friends who are so close that even though it might be years between times we see each other, we can pick up as though it were yesterday. How blessed I am!

I received a "card" from someone in Montana. The return address gave the last name "Cole." I didn't know any "Coles" in Montana so it really stirred my curiosity. I responded to the card asking who the person was, where they got my address, were we related? Another fascinating story. I was friends with another writer, who communicated with this "Cole" in Montana. One day, she noticed communication from two "Coles," and decided to put them together. Most of my life as a pastor's wife I felt disoriented from other "pastor's wives." I just never seemed to come up to their level of spiritually. Also, we'd always had a small church, so I never "clicked" with the larger, more "organized or sophisticated" places of worship. Soon, the two Coles were on the pone with each other. I was asking, "How large is your Church?" Her answer, "we have about 10-15 most Sundays. Hmmmmmm. That sure sounded like she might be "like minded." She also taught a women's Bible study group. They lived on the border of a "Crow" Indian reservation and sometimes two or three of the Indian ladies would come. Wow! At Thanksgiving, the Indian leaders would prepare buffalo and give to the pastor's Church family. The more I learned, the more fascinating it was. I realized the Lord had gone all the way to Montana to find a pastor's wife that could be a friend to me. Oh! What love! Later, I received a very heavy package from Montana. In the box was a ***brick*** with the name "Cole" engraved on one side. I know. These coincidences are overlapping each other. It seems this family had lived in Texas, and when they decided to redo their kitchen, they found bricks, all stamped with the name Cole, the company that produced them.

Like passion, I wonder about the emptiness of those who don't have friends. I don't know how to tell you to "get there," but the Word says that if you want a friend, be a friend.

Several years ago a family of five came to our church and the man of the house led worship. He was not a musician, but he was a worshipper and blessed us for several years. Even though they moved to another state, they stay in touch. Dan preached the funeral of his father and his grandmother, and performed the wedding for his niece. A couple of weeks after Dan passed away, the niece came to church holding a Bible. She said Dan had given it to her dad and when he passed away, her grandmother gave it to her. She had just become a believer, and studied all the notes in the columns of the Bible. As she held the Bible up for all to see, she explained how precious it was to her. God is so good.

CHAPTER FOURTEEN

BRANCHES OF THE TREE PERSONALITIES FOR WHICH I HAVE NO ANSWERS

Through the years as our children grew up, and their personalities developed, "our passion" almost took a sideline to the anger and frustrations experienced by the children. The dream of the perfect family disappeared as the boys left home—going in different directions with differing goals.

Jay was never a happy child. ***Most, if not all*** of that was my fault, and his childhood was horrendous. I was too young to understand his confusion and his troubled, complex personality. He was destructive and I was abusive. We worked against each other at every level. It was when he was little that I began taking tranquilizers to "cope." It didn't change him, but numbed me. He was often in trouble in school, even though he was quite brilliant. He was at a difficult age when his father and I divorced and that was yet another trauma for him.

Jay just never settled, and had a series of horrible "mishaps." He went to live with his father soon after Dan and my marriage, then he had an accident that left his leg so damaged he still suffers with it. He ran away from his father's house shortly thereafter. He wandered about the country during the time of communes when unhappy young people lived together. He wore a cast for a long time and I remember he came to visit us at the chicken farm and rode our horse, Blaze, with that cast covering his leg. I've told you about the incident when he was sent home from California after getting in trouble there. For a long time, I didn't know where he was, but every now and then, he'd call and "check in." During that time, he was able to master some computer skills and so has been able to earn a living. He's been a trapper—a hunter, an award winning fisherman, and a talented photographer.

You know, we change all the time, we've talked about that. But Jay was outside the changes that were going on within our family—at Trout Creek and the chicken farm, and later, on Minnow Creek. Jay was an angry young man and I hold the blame for so much of it. He expressed his rage by burning down the gazebo we built at Trout Creek—some time after we had moved. He made wrong choices based on his anger and rejection I think. He felt I had abandoned him and he had every reason to think that. It's a terrible thing for a young man to feel rejected and abandoned by his own mother. I have surely grieved for causing that pain and anguish in his life.

For a long time, we reflect the hurts and turmoil of our childhood. We make choices based on those experiences. But sooner or later, we must take responsibility for those decisions.

One of my friends mentioned in the "friends chapter" showed so much wisdom when she and her husband separated. She talked to her sons and explained that she loved them and the separation had nothing to do with them. I wasn't that wise. I was lost in a maze of love's delirium. I truly was blind with passion and couldn't comprehend what was going on in the minds and spirits of my young sons. But years afterward, I still haven't had "that conversation" with them. Much to my shame.

When I worked at the police department, a dear friend told me one time that she had seen each of the boys "in their personalities." Jay was open with his actions, which were not always right but never hidden. David was quiet and you never knew what he was about. Craig was a fun loving, sweet boy who just enjoyed life. Those descriptions have held true throughout the years.

Craig served some time in the military, then he went to work for the post office, like his birth father. He's married with three daughters and four grandchildren. Craig has a heart to serve the Lord and has served as an elder in several churches in the west coast as far as Alaska. He loves the body of Christ and is happily married.

David, the quiet one, went into the military and became a part of the elite special operations unit and retired. After traveling all over the world, he chose to settle down just north of my home and we are able to stay in touch—even more so as I age. David has two children and four grandchildren and we stay in touch and spent time together. Jay does computer work and continues to live life on the edge.

Interestingly, David and Jay both have attributes like Dan. They ride motorcycles, like the outdoors and fish, hunt or grow their vegetables. Craig, doesn't fish, doesn't ride, and enjoys *views* of the ocean, while digging his toes deep in the sane as he hunts for shells. When he lived in the northwest, he spent many years taking long bicycle rides. They're grown men, but they still carry the trauma that has affected their lives and personalities.

CHAPTER FIFTEEN

PASSION & TENACITY

Passion + tenacity = a finished work. God promises to complete the work He begins in each one of us.

Like Paul, when it was necessary, Dan was a "tent-maker."

But going back a few years—that's what we're doing, right?—Dan worked for a tiny little woman manager of a condominium doing maintenance work. That included the simplest to the most complicated types of "maintenance," including changing washers on faucets, and light bulbs. No matter what the job, the little lady "stood over him" to make he was doing it right. One day he came home exasperated. "I cleaned 42 toilets today," he sighed.

He was a full time pastor for fifteen years. During that period of time, he didn't do any secular work. But along about that 15th year, he felt he was supposed to take on an outside, part time job. There was no "apparent" reason for me. The Church was taking care of us, and we were living comfortably.

Dan was hired by a golf course doing maintenance—in the shop where the mechanics kept the machines running, and the blades sharpened. Greasy, dirty, and with the added "filth radio," his responsibility was to clean up behind the mechanics. They learned soon enough that he was a pastor, and they responded accordingly. They blasted the vulgarity of the radio, threw cigarette butts at his feet, used the most vile language, and just generally tried to "get his goat." But his goat was tied to the cross and there was no "loosening" it. He prayed. We were confused. If a righteous man's steps are "ordered by the Lord," then what was this all about?

The passion Dan had for the Lord caused him to do his best to be a living example of Jesus as he worked in this hostile environment. For a long time it seemed nothing would change. He continued to live his life. Slowly, the men began to show some respect for this gentle man of God in little ways, like tossing the butts into the barrel instead of at his feet. The language and attitude didn't seem to change, but before too long, one of the worse offenders left and went to work elsewhere. He had been the one to play "smut radio," argue with Dan at every opportunity, and always used the filthiest profanity. We counted his leaving a real blessing.

A young man who used to work in that shop was here helping Chip yesterday. As he worked, he told one story after another about Dan and how tenacious he was. "He'd never give up," he said.

"He'd stay with a job until it was done, and done right," he explained. "If he didn't have a tool, he'd make one. He was quite the guy. There'll never be another one like him." Dan created a love bone with the men with whom he worked . . . if they were open. For a few years, there were more men attending our church than women. He identified with them. He was not religious, not "holier than thou," and he was a man's man. They were quick to recognize that.

Eventually, Dan was promoted to foreman of the shop and there were some men who felt they deserved that promotion and were upset. The last time that happened was when we worked on the chicken farm. The man who thought he was supposed to be prompted spit in Dan's face, he was so angry. Dan explained to him that God had made a change in his life and had he not been born again, he would have, in his words, "decked him." His passion for the Lord tenaciously determined that he live the life no matter what anyone threw at him.

Then the Church "emptied." Musicians, teachers, "members," just left. All at once. One Sunday Dan and I stood outside the door of the Church and Dan said, "All we have to offer is Jesus. If that's not enough, we'll be here alone. But I'm not going anywhere. I know God put me here, and here I'll stay."

During the next few years people came and went, receiving what they needed and then moving on. It was eerie, but we had a peace that was strangely satisfying. Dan's passion was in obedience. It was said at his funeral that the success of his ministry was in his obedience to do whatever God told him to do. Like David, God knew that Dan, too, was a man after God's own heart, "because he would do whatever God told him to do."

CHAPTER SIXTEEN

"IT'S TIME!"

One Sunday morning, as we rushed about getting ready for church, I realized I didn't know where Dan was. The garage door was up, which meant he was loading the car. It was a "first Sunday" and I had "covered dishes" to take. I didn't see him, and assumed he was watering his many "posies." Finally, I went into his office to get a hole-punch, and found him slumped at his desk. At some point in the morning, he had gently slipped away into the arms of Jesus. When I saw his "earth suit" as he called it, I recognized immediately that he had left it behind and he was not there. My lover of over 42 years had left without saying good-bye.

In the following days, I realized he had said his good-byes in many ways. He took his sailboat out and went fishing and was excited to have "caught supper." He cleaned them in my kitchen sink. I asked, "Are you going to clean those fish in my kitchen sink?" [I suddenly had taken total possession of it!] "Yes, I am," was his quiet response. Not like him. He always cleaned the fish outside. I fried the fish and it was delicious. "Fish are best when fresh caught," he'd always say.

We had a date every Friday for as long as I can remember. So when he told me on a Wednesday that he wanted a Cuban sandwich, I just figured I'd lost out on my date night. We went to a local Cuban restaurant and he was a happy man.

When Friday came, I had planned to baby sit our two granddaughters about an hour and a half away. He noticed I had a flat tire. He called the auto repair shop and insisted they put a new tire on the car immediately. Not like him. He pumped it up and drove it to get the tire. I was getting ready to leave and he asked, "Are you ready for our date?" I was packed, but sensed I needed to stop and go for our dinner date. We talked. I don't remember what we talked about but it was good.

I got back Saturday afternoon and he was sitting on the loveseat in our bedroom. He didn't get up, like he usually did, to help bring in the things from the car. I nagged him, "Hey! Look at me! I'm unloading the car!" But he didn't respond. As we sat there watching a movie, his hand slipped into mine and that same tingle from his touch was sweet. I was loved as few women are and I knew it. I thought it would last forever. But in the next 24 hours I was swept into a new and unknown world. The world called "widow." . . . .

Our son whisked me away to his home and Craig flew down to be with us. It was a joy to have him. Even in those circumstances. But it was a difficult time. Like the members of the

"Enterprise," I entered a space I had never gone before. Like most women, I wasn't "myself." I don't know what I was. It was a surreal world. The ladies from Church took over all the memorial service preparations, and did a lovely job of it. From my son's home, I made whatever decisions that needed my specific instruction. The precious ladies of the church did the running. Those days are a blur, of course, but soon I began to see somewhat clearly. I say 'somewhat," because months, later, I'm still "not right."

Hannah, who was three, was my constant comfort. I told her "up front" that I needed lots of hugs, so when our eyes would make contact, one of us would tell the other, "It's time." That meant, of course, to rush to each other and get a desperately needed hug. Hannah has a gentle spirit and she was "just what I needed." I still do. It's been over three years, but Sunday, after Church we went to lunch. That precious little girl looked across the table from me and said, "Grandma, it's time." Oh, yes! No better "time."

I have bouts of sobbing, sometimes uncontrollable. I don't understand what plans the Lord has for my life. After forty two years of married life, of a life shared in ministry, what does one do as a "widow?" Who on earth created that word anyway? What does it mean? As I sit here, I realize that **most of my friends are widows.** I've watched them go through the passing, the loss, the confusion, the emptiness. They've all responded differently. Some of them have been left with small children to raise alone. Others, are still mourning "what they never had." Me? I still have "things" surrounding me. That complex, tender-hearted giant of a man had multiple passions.

He built radio controlled airplanes and prided himself on creating original plans, and building everything from huge "big birds" to small, transparent planes. I have one of those hanging in my bedroom right now. He spent hours in the most intricate details and each plane stood on its own as a well crafted reproduction that would fly perfectly.

Everything he did was with precision. He never "skipped a step," whether he was scraping barnacles, painting his sailboat, caring for the yard and his many "posies," or making love.

When Dan passed away, there was an emptiness I had never experienced. Following some extraordinary experiences in the church family, and many wrong choices made by me, the nucleus or core group of our church left. We did not have another minister prepared to carry on that responsibility and there were differences of opinions about that as well.

There were many decisions to make and I learned later that my son expected me to lean on him for direction, etc. So there were a few disasters and many of them had high prices to pay—and not just financially. The last months have been harsh and stressful and have left me with some pretty serious physical consequences. But God is faithful. My son is now the pastor of the Church, blessed with wisdom and discernment. He knows he 's exactly where he belongs and he knows he's where God has placed him. He has such a peace about it, he encourages me every day. But for the first time in over forty years, I am in a new position altogether, in ministry, my personal and family life. It's a new day with new challenges and it's both exciting and startling. That seed is still there, pushing upward with new buds, and promises of more blooms. That, my friend, is passion.

My husband *lived* a life of passion. From the moment he accepted Jesus as his Savior, he had a passion to know Him in an intimate relationship and that caused him to dig deep into the Bible. He truly wanted to "know him"—that same word, "know," is used in the intimacies of the marriage bond. Remembering what that "feels" like is this: You want to be as close as possible to the one you love. You want to be with him every minute. You want to read anything he's written to you—a note taped to the fridge or a love letter to far away Alaska. You don't want to miss a word he says. You want to read the same books so you can discuss them. You just want to be as close as possible as long as possible. That's what a lifetime commitment is all about.

That doesn't mean just staying together in the same house. Dan used to call that "in house divorce."

He also had a tremendous passion for fishing. It would build and build. He couldn't go very long without getting out on the water. And, he explained to me, fishing is not just about catching fish. You can enjoy a wonderful day on the water *just fishing for fish whether you ever catch a fish or not.* He flew his radio-controlled planes when weather permitted. He enjoyed the thrill to be able to fly a plane he built with his own hands.

Another of Dan's passions was classical music. We had season tickets to the local symphony. The orchestra is made up of older, seasoned musicians and young students from the high school. The last season we went, a young student cellist caught our attention because he kept a big grin on his face throughout the symphony. At the break, I asked him what he was so happy about. "What's not to love with this tremendous music. I love it all.—the musicians, the instruments, the work that goes into such lovely compositions. I just love it. It makes me very happy."

Tears began to flow as soon as the rather large audience stood at attention responding to the spotlight focusing on the American flag. In the darkened room, a respectful hush filled the theatre. We stood together and sang "God Bless America." Dan was moved so strongly he usually just sat and sobbed through the whole concert. The rich compositions touched him deeply. We began every Christmas morning by playing Handel's Messiah. He has always loved the work, but a few years ago, a contemporary Christian group performed it in a large Church auditorium. The seats for the concert were immediately sold out so they arranged a second concert the following night and it too, was sold out!

Popular contemporary musicians played the anointed selections, performing the solos with their fresh young voices, the rasping voice of Phil Driscoll and exceptional electric guitars played by he and Phil Keaggy. Dan loved it . . . and cried. Of course.

CHAPTER SEVENTEEN

WORDS OF PASSION

He licked the spoon after dipping it in a jar of peanut butter and I quickly warned him, "Don't put the spoon back in the jar!!!" He answered quietly, "It would be no different than kissing you!" My heart pounded. I caught my breath. Scene: it was in the middle of the booking desk at the Tampa Police Station. They were the first words we had exchanged. And I'll never forget them.

"I knew you wanted me to kiss you," he whispered. That was a memory of over 40 years ago. We were sitting quietly one evening sharing some of those early memories of the many passionate days and nights so long ago. Like a child who says, "Read it again," or "Tell me again," I loved to listen to those memories repeated over and over. But this was the first time he revealed to me that he knew the passion in my spirit was longing for his lips to touch mine.

Not long after that, he confessed, "I'm glad you're home, safe and sound." I returned from an overnight visit to care for the grandchildren. Less than twenty four hours later, he was gone. I had no clue he was so close to death. But I think he knew.

"Do you know how I cherish you?" he asked as I walked by. There was no conversation going on. We were just having a quiet evening together at home. My heart skipped a beat and for a minute or two, again, I was breathless. Does *anyone* understand the passion experienced by people our age? Does the passion lessen because your skin sags, or id discolored, or it becomes harder and harder to stand after sitting for a while? Or your step is slow and your sight or hearing is impaired? *True passion endures all the changes.* It's altered a little, perhaps, but only a little. It's still deep within. The interesting thing is that it grows over the years as we deal with life situations. In the beginning, there's a lot of flesh involved. Not to worry! God put all those sensitive erogenous zones there. *He put them there. [See "The Wedding Gift" by Geri Cole—published by Publish America 2003].* As we go through the hurts, learn the imperative of forgiveness, we grow and mature. We learn that "a believer can't *afford* the *luxury* of unforgiveness." The heartbreaks heal and the things we've done to hurt one another eventually settle into obscurity. Those tell tale creases show up, and our heart sometimes becomes weak. We grieve for the one we love because of the things we did or said to hurt them. We even learn to forgive ourselves eventually.

Here comes another wave—He planted over a hundred pansies along the sidewalk leading to the front door. "When you look at them, I want you to remember that each one cries out, "I love you!" I planted them this year—without him. But they still cry out, "I love you," and that passionate tenderness flows over me like a gentle breeze.

Sitting at the kitchen table, I gave him the first few pages of this book. "Oh!" he said, almost gasping. "Are you okay?" I quickly asked.

"The Lord just spoke to me and said this book is anointed."

I hope you are experiencing that anointing. I know that passion, itself, is a gift from God. He gives and gives and gives. But not everyone is ready to receive. I could refer back to all He has promised in the Word. He died, but not everyone has accepted that as personal payment for their sins. He rose again, but not everyone can accept that He's alive forevermore.

Sitting with his guitar at his side, Dan looked around the family room. People from our home church group had met every week for a shared meal, some worship and Bible study. It was the time we used to celebrate—*anything*. Quietly—he was the ultimate "quiet man"—Dan expressed his love for this group. "You know I love each one of you very much." They weren't just "words," he was tenderly exposing his heart. Each of us knew it and welcomed his affection. Every now and then, he would do the same thing as he spoke to the congregation at Church. When he spoke those words, they penetrated into each heart. Often, there were people listening who had spoken against him, criticized him, complained against him, murmured like the children of Israel, etc. But he allowed Jesus' love and forgiveness to pour out of him and into their spirits. *They knew he meant it.* But maybe they didn't know how he had to be taught to forgive the offenses so he *could truly* love them. He carried God's passion around inside. Ready. Instant in season and out. Ready to forgive. Ready to love. Ready to comfort. Ready to listen. Ready to be still and understand. Ready to respond with a tender touch.

"I love you, brother," he said quietly to a fellow mechanic in the privacy of his office. These two big men, greasy and garbed in mechanic's uniforms, held on to each other as one cried out for mercy to the Lord. That happened often. There were no barriers to his open love and compassion.

At the end of July, we celebrated Hannah's fourth birthday. A breeze blew through the tall trees that surrounded their home. A fence bordered the above ground pool with its deck and beautifully landscaped back yard. The girls learned to swim while still little, and Lily became an absolute fish right away. She swam underwater, and begged her daddy to toss her in the air; he gladly obliged.

At her party, little Hannah decided to dress as a princess. She wore her crown proudly and her long, fluffy dress enhanced her "regal" position. Along with many gifts, she received a toy "hair dryer" as a present. That sweet passion poured over me as her grampa yielded to, "Let me dry your hair, Grampa." I watched him lean over so Hannah could "dry" his very thin hair. He had become weak but he loved his little granddaughters. Love's passion pours out in many directions. It is *felt*. It is *experienced. It flows over your whole being. It's never the same, but always irresistible.*

The grandchildren were spending the night. We were "working" at entertaining them. They wanted to play hide and seek—inside the house. Dan hid in the closet near the front door—this giant of a man with the tender spirit. "I found you! I found you!" little Hannah squealed. It was the best of games. My heart overflowed with the love this gentle man showed to his little granddaughters.

I told Hannah I was writing another book. *"Is this one about Grampa, too?"* She asked. "Of course it is! Who else?"

CHAPTER EIGHTEEN

WATCHING PASSION DEVELOP

Chip has a passion for music. When he was growing up, he didn't watch television, and there was no computer. He spent hours in his room practicing the guitar. As a youngster, he played the snare drum and marched with his school band. He also played with our church ministry on a local beach. Later, he learned the bass guitar, then acoustic and electric guitar. A musician friend has said when he hears Chip play, he just wants to turn his own guitar into a planter. Chip is a good example of how passion affects our behavior. He went to Christian school and played in the worship team. He played with the worship team at our Church. At nineteen, he learned about a Christian tour group that was hiring musicians. He applied and was soon off to band camp, where he was told he needed to read music. Since he didn't know how, he was told if he wanted to tour with the group he would have to learn and was given two weeks to accomplish that assignment. For two weeks, he studied alone in a room—and *taught himself to read music. That's passion.*

As a youngster, he dreamed of playing before thousands and before the summer ended, he had achieved that dream. He experienced playing for school assemblies and later having girls follow him around and give him teddy bears and other gifts. The tour group played and performed for every kind of audience—state fairs, conventions, festivals, theme parks, and they were constantly "on the move." Since Chip was the last one hired, he was expected to do all the driving. He had never left Florida, so driving through sleet and snow, through the northwest, where he drove miles without seeing anything but wildlife, was God's gift of adventure to him. He went on to play with other Christian groups, performed in restaurants and bars, and his dad and I went to all the strange places to encourage him. God had placed that seed of passion deep within him. When he was growing up, his dad led worship, played the guitar and violin, and music was an integral part of his life.

I had a mother's fear that if he were playing in places that served liquor, where people danced and slobbered over each other, somehow it didn't "seem" to be good for a fine Christian boy's "image." The Lord gave me a real peace about it, letting me know that he was learning things he would never learn anywhere else. And so he did.

When he was performing at a prestigious restaurant on a river north of us, Chip met the girl who became his wife. He had experienced some heart breaks, and finally confessed that American girls were just not mature enough for him. He guessed he would have to go to Europe to find a wife. Just as it happened in the Bible, God selected a wife from far, far away and brought her to him. Zuzana was from Slovakia and hadn't been in the country very long when they met. Sometimes Zuzana sang with him, and always encouraged him. But God had a call on his life and a reason for the passion. One day, he received a flyer in the mail advertising an audition for musicians to form a worship team for a Church nearby. He auditioned and played there for a couple of years, even leading worship. But that was still preparation for what the Lord had for him. In each situation, he was learning valuable lessons he would need later.

The seed kept struggling to burst into bloom. It is blossoming as he stepped into the role of pastor two years ago.

Big brown eyes. Long dark brown hair. A tender spirit ready to reach out to Jesus. When did it all begin? Lily and Hannah, my two granddaughters, were as different as could possibly be. Lily, tall and slim with long legs like her dad, was wiry and bright. She was quick and continually winning honors at school. She never stopped. She was reading in kindergarten, and mastering the computer soon after. I guess in today's world that's not so unusual *but it was amazing to me!*

Often, when I was sleeping over, we'd play that game so familiar with my cousins and me years before. We'd "draw" pictures on each other's backs and guess what they were. Sometimes, I'd interject a story about their Grampa, and the rich things he said and the love God poured out through him. They were always fascinated. Today they can repeat the stories word for word.

Hamsters? When we lived on the chicken farm, we had hamsters. Two. The wrong "two." Soon we had thirteen. After waiting the required time after their births, I took the "habitrail" apart to clean it. It had a tall cylinder that slid into a "penthouse." When I put it back together I wasn't careful to make sure the parts locked together, and the cylinder fell across the back of one of the tiny babies. He lay spread out and looked dead. Dan was having coffee with a friend at the table just a few feet from the habitrail, and when that happened, we looked at each other with a "My God can do all things," knowing. So I grabbed the little thing and laid it on the table. Without a word spoken, Dan touched the little back and announced, "His back is broken in two places." The visitor said, "Well you have plenty of 'em left!" But Dan and I were both praying quietly that God would touch the back and heal him. He did that very thing.

In a very short time, the little animal got up on all fours and tried to run off the table. "Oh! He wasn't hurt at all!" the guy commented. We knew that wasn't true. We didn't need to explain it away. We prayed believing, and God answered the prayer.

Looking at my old, discolored and wrinkled hands, Hannah commented about my engagement and wedding rings. As soon as I began "the story," Lily jumped in: "Grampa took you to a Chinese restaurant and he prayed over the food. He held your hand while he was praying, and put the ring on your finger." Yes, that's exactly the way it happened and I know it has become real to them.

Hannah was full of giggles, but early on, there was a sensitivity in her spirit. I don't know when it began, but when the family move din with me after Dan's death, and as they were preparing to move into a home near me, I noticed that it was Hannah who prayed at meals, and at the slightest nudge that there was a need.

Soon, when she prepared for bed, she'd slip into my room with that, "It's time, Grandma." She'd put her arms around me and pray. Sometimes, she'd suggest I pray first, other times she'd begin. She had an amazing memory, and always remembered to pray for those in serious need, like my friend's son, who was in the military. We prayed that the angels would protect him and his company, and even asked the Lord to let them see the angels who were helping them. I surely expected that to happen!

She had quickly moved past the "God is great . . . ." and talked to the Lord personally. Last night I got a call from a mother who was distressed about her daughter. When I hung up, I called Hannah to my room. "We need to pray," I told her. She quickly came to where I was sitting and put her arms around me. "A mother called for us to pray for her daughter," I explained to her. Immediately, Hannah began to pay that God touch her and make her mother feel better. I know God hears children's prayers, but there was certainly no doubt at that moment.

However, right now, she's jumping on her daddy, after he has worked in the rain all day. I knows he loves it.

Where does that passion begin? How? Is it in the infancy of a heart's cry as she's developing inside her mother? As she heard her daddy pray? We've known for a long time that early in a baby's development an infant hears and responds to the sounds outside the mother's body. I heard a man yesterday say that when his wife was pregnant, they played different kinds of music to see what the baby's reaction would be. Surprise, surprise, she slept [or at least got quiet] when she heard Tony Bennett. We've also read that Japanese babies are exposed to classical music, reading from classical literature, etc.

There was a couple who were very faithful to our church, coming to all the services. The baby inside got very familiar with the voices. The day he was born, we went to see the family. When my husband spoke, the baby turned toward him, recognizing his familiar voice. Let this be a reminder to be sensitive about our words and music when near anyone's developing baby.

But there is a negative aspect to this whole thing. An infant who hears his parents talk about not being able to afford a baby, or a parent saying they don't want him, often takes on rejection. When the baby is born, no matter how much the child is loved and touched, hugged and kissed, that child carries the rejection. It develops and affects the personality and causes him to act out because of it. *That needs to be dealt with in prayer.* God can remove it forever. Just ask Him how.

CHAPTER NINETEEN

Unrequited Love

We had a glorious memorial service for Dan. The church was overflowing—literally—with friends, family and loved ones who cam from near and far to show their love and respect for him. The love that he had planted in those people's lives saturated the very walls of our small Church.

The following Sunday we were back to square one. A tiny group of people met for the Sunday morning service. Dan used to say, "They love our but . . . ." because whenever someone was going to leave the church *they always said "I love you . . . . but." [We need to move on, we feel "led" somewhere else, etc.]*

Was our love not returned? It's been a question we have lived with for all the years we've served the Lord. It seemed we poured out our love and affection only to be rejected over and over again, Unrequited love.

If it weren't the passion we shared about this little Church and the conviction that God had put us there and we were to say until He moved us or took us away, we would have run screaming from the scene many times. But the passion in our hearts for God's gracious gift held us close to Him even when nearly everyone else left us. We understood how Paul felt when he mentioned that all had left him. We can sense the rejection when he explains that "only Luke" was with him.

A friend explained our passion. She said, "This Church was birthed by your love for the Lord and each other." What a sweet thought. A love child.

In these days, it's hard to find anyone who has a passion to serve God in any capacity. There is little commitment and people don't seem to take the gospel seriously. Many are more interested in the entertainment and activities than the gospel of Jesus Christ. The Blood has not lost its power; instead, people have allowed their ears to be deafened by the world.

When I went into the hospital earlier this summer, I was home for a couple of days before I was back again. I received an email from another old friend who gave me this word: **"This sickness is not unto death. The Lord wants to heal your broken heart. He wants to heal years of pile-ups of disappointments and bring a deep refreshing to you. He asks you to quiet your**

heart before him and let Him access those places, even long forgotten, and He will surely heal and refresh you for a new season of fruitfulness."

I receive that encouraging word. I want to enjoy what time remains of my life. And I want to understand this "unrequited love" I have felt. I think that in our passions, Dan and I have always given completely of ourselves to everyone we've been close to. We've given of our love sacrificially. Well, Dan has, anyway. He has always h ad a more tender heart than me. Because of that, he has been more deeply hurt and experienced more rejection. Our Church has always been a family. The believers come as babes, study the Word, begin to grow and mature, and then they're ready to go on, and they do. Each time they "leave home" we go into an empty next syndrome. Someone reminded me that *they're not your children. They're God's children, and He can put them wherever He wants them."* True, but the heartaches come anyway. Someone has said, *"You just get too close to everyone."*

We didn't know how not to.

This is a time when we need to be in prayer that God would raise up men and women, boys and girls, who will have a passion to serve Him. A passion to lay down their lives for the gospel's sake. People in other parts of the world are experiencing that passion and many are losing their lives because they dare to stand fast in their belief. When Dan water baptized people, he always asked the question, "If it meant your death, would you still follow Jesus?"

I used to think that was a bit strong, but now I know the Word is very clear about the statistics of those who will be saved and those who will not. It's a serious thing to take a stand for Jesus. We used to sing an old hymn, "I'll go with Him, with Him, all the way." That "all the way" sometimes takes us to broken hearts and misunderstandings. It takes us to places where we feel disoriented and rejected—as though we've lost our way. We feel distanced from the One we love and His people.

When "The Passion of the Christ" (a few years ago made as a very popular film) is mentioned, it refers to the unconditional love that caused Jesus to give Himself over to the torturers and the angry mob. Because of His passionate, intimate love for each of us, He took upon Himself every sin, every sickness and all rejection, in our place.

The bud of passion is alive and well. Sometimes it seems to lie dormant, but we can be sure it can and will be revived. The hunger for intimacy with the Lover of our souls reaches out by His Spirit and draws us to Himself.

CHAPTER TWENTY

INTERNATIONAL PASSION

One of our favorite places to eat was a local Chinese restaurant. We went often, in fact, Dan took me there for a "date" a few days before he passed away. Lots of memories there. One day, as we sat in the booth, Dan, wearing suspenders, felt a sudden 'snap!" against his back. A tiny young Chinese server was the culprit. It seemed highly unusual that a person of that culture would be so personal. When we turned to see her, a big smile filled her countenance. That was the beginning of an unexplainable relationship. "Bobo" couldn't speak any English and lived in unbelievable circumstances, but she was determined to communicate. Somehow, she obtained a hand held computer that translated English to Chinese and visa versa. And so began a sweet bond between us.

One Sunday, when we came in after Church, she drew a building with a steeple on a napkin. She was asking if we had been to Church. She let us know she had seen a movie about Jesus, shown outdoors in China. She showed us her cell phone with pictures of her two young children. Her grandparents had taken them back to China after they were born so Bobo and her husband (a cook) could work here and send money home. I can't believe the loss she must have felt, but she compensated somewhat by adopting us as grandparents.

Conversations were many and once we even left the restaurant forgetting to pay the bill. Dan suddenly turned around the returned, only to see Bobo standing near the door with that big grin. *She never gave us the bill. She paid it herself.*

Her blouse that was part of her uniform was wrinkled and we checked to see if she needed any (other) clothes. She did and we approached the ladies of our church who gave and gave their tiny (sizes 0-2) clothing. They even included shirts, etc. for her husband, a Buddhist. She shared with the young people who worked with her (and lived with her and her husband). They were all thrilled. They lived with all the young people who worked together in one small, cramped house. It was near the restaurant and they took turns working and sleeping. And they all walked to work.

I can't explain the affect of that relationship. The restaurant company moved the young people from one restaurant to another all over the country. And so one day, when we went, she wasn't there. We've exchanged phone calls but never saw her again. She sent us a big box of things from China—love gifts. What she gave us in that loving grin will never be forgotten. We include her in family photos and as I write this, I see her beautiful smile across the room looking at me with a love unparalleled.

The next time we were at the buffet an older Chinese woman came from the kitchen and gave us a big hug. She motioned for us to "stay" while she returned to the kitchen for a container. She handed it to us with a loving expression. It was a pot of soup, and we cherished that love gift. Bobo's love for us had touched this woman visibly.

CHAPTER TWENTY-ONE

THE PASSION OF GRIEF

Alone. More than "lonely," the emptiness is overwhelming. For years we were known as Dan and Geri, one name never mentioned without the other. A flood of emotions filled each day as I stayed with my son and his family that first week. I can't remember, still, the life spent during those days. I had given Dan a small photo album just a couple of weeks before he died, and I do remember I took it with me. I don't remember taking anything else but I know I did that. Hannah and I looked at the little album and cried often. We cried about *our loss*, and the clichés spoken to encourage never did. I know there is nothing that can be said to alleviate the loss, or take away the pain, but I know, too, that those who loved Dan were just sharing their own grief, wit hopes that ours would be lessened.

It's been three years since Dan left. I still feel his touch, the warmth of his embrace, his constant caring and protection. Left alone, without his guidance, I've made so many wrong choices and decisions. I miss his guidance and wisdom. I miss his *presence*. There's on one to fill that huge gap. There's no one with whom to share my daily life. There's just *missing him*.

I especially miss him when something *breaks*. He could fix *anything. And he did*. Now, it's a new day with new circumstances. I had a flat tire in the middle of a busy highway the other day. Feeling sorry for myself, I just cried and it didn't help at all. Then I got mad at Dan for *not being there for me*. I don't like to watch TV on the loveseat we shared. I miss his hand touching mine. I miss everything about him.

I get mad at all the things I have to do myself because he's not there. The clichés that "he's in a better place," etc, just don't work for me.

Every now and then I see someone who looks like him walking toward me. I know it's not him, but I catch my breath anyway. I hear music that I know would cause him to sob and I'm careful not to watch movies that I know would stir his emotions. I don't watch fishing shows or MASH, or action movies. I emptied out his office (actually my son moved the office to the attic—I'll probably never find some of those things). I still go to that room looking for something from his desk, etc.

When asked soon after his leaving if I were going to stay in this house—in their opinion surely too much house for me, I wonder, "Why? Why would I want to leave a place where every room, every niche, has memories?"

CHAPTER TWENTY-TWO

THE PASSION OF CHANGE

I'm recovering from cancer and sitting here in my family room, I face a window that looks out at the branches of a huge bamboo tree. Multitudes of birds fly in and out. This morning as I watched the birds dart here and there—swooping down for some work or such—In noticed a bright color—bright golden yellow—as it left the branch to float down to earth. The sun is shining through the morning leaves which have a touch of dawn's dew and they glisten with color and joy. The leaves are developing different hues as they, one by one, enter this time of *change*. Change is not a bad thing. It's just that "next step." As those leaves drop off, something else is happening. The tree is taking on a *transparency*. That is, now you can see the sky beyond the limbs. Soon, there will be no leaves left hanging and the fullness of the sun will shine through the emptiness. The once cooling shade of the tree will now be transformed into warmth for the chill of winter days. *Change is part of the overall plan.* It's a good thing.

Last year, my son, Chip, came by the house. He opened the conversation with, "Mom, this is probably the hardest thing I've had to do as pastor." He then explained that his brother in Arkansas had called to ask him to come over and relay the heartbreaking information that my second son, David, had died suddenly at age 54. David had been so close to me in recent days. The announcement was surreal. Since leaving the military, David had bought a home in a fishing town north of where I live. He soon went to work with some commercial fishermen who stayed out for days and sometimes, weeks. The boat, with a full load of fish, had docked the night before, and the captain decided to wait until morning to unload the pounds of fish and ice. In the morning, as they were dealing with the large quantity, David suddenly told the skipper he wasn't feeling well. That was very unusual for him, and the response was, "Well, we're almost done. But David was already "done." He collapsed and was gone at that moment.

Immediately the plan of the day disappeared. Usually, when David came into port, he called and we made arrangements for a lunch out. Usually at some exotic place and I looked forward to it. There is a Greek community nearby and we both enjoyed going there. [I learned that "Greek spaghetti" was not the same as Italian.] He treated me like a "date," and I soaked it up.

During the horrors of "the summer from hell," with all the near death experiences, David was there. He was single, and free to take me to doctor's appointments, staying with me while the medical people tortured me, trying to insert a port for the long term IVs. He was with me and overseeing my treatment in Tampa as different procedures were accomplished. He brought me home, stopping along the way for a Mexican supper. He stayed overnight for the rest of the week, making sure I had medication, food to eat, and a fun movie to watch. Now, suddenly that would never happen again.

Things were revealed at his funeral that were revelations to me. David retired from the military after serving with special ops, but he never quite "found himself" in civilian life. He spent his time and efforts in giving to others, and as different ones related all he had been to them, I was proud and surprised at their stories. One particularly striking account was about his long hair. When he went into the military at 18, he had long thick hair. That disappeared quickly. But when he retired, he let it grow again. One day, he came by and that long hair was gone. I learned at the funeral that he had given it to be used for cancer patients how had lost their hair.

In the midst of sharing at the funeral, one scruffy old man stood and told the story: 'I was out of work for three months. During that time, David paid my mortgage and brought food to the house for my family and me." Oh! What love; what a generous spirit!!! David was involved in many of the national service organizations and they were well represented that day. I cherish the flag, folded and presented to me, and even more, the memories revealed about my son.

For over thirty years, I walked hand in hand with my pastor husband. Now that he was gone, I suffered a real "identity crisis." For a while, I wasn't sure who I was or what was expected of me. Looking back, it seemed I walked in circles a lot and kept "running into myself."

During these days and months I had a revelation of how susceptible widows are snatched up by charming con men. I had read the stories of women being robbed blind (and willingly!!) by that type who swooped in on vulnerable lonely women and never could understand how it could happen. Now I do.

How could "passion" enter into these changes? It is passion that holds you close no matter what the situation you're enduring.

TWENTY-THREE

THE PASSION OF SACRIFICE

My husband walked in that passion of sacrifice. Over and over, he gave of himself. It was not at all unusual, when someone commented on a guitar he was playing, that he would just give it to them. Was that sacrifice? Or was it just "who he was?"

When we lived on the chicken farm, a little girl up the dirt road from us asked for a ride to church. Dan was glad to do it, and each Sunday morning, he would drive through the rain, jumping the potholes, and up the winding road to her house. Most of the time, she had "slept over" at a friend's house, or hadn't gotten up, or worse, changed her mind and didn't want to go at all. In questioning his reasons for going through all the agony, he realized that if he was doing it to please the Lord, the Lord would let him know if He wanted him to stop. He did, too.

We had an old friend who was also a "giver" and often would go to local farms and pick strawberries, blueberries, corn, etc. and then, clean and deliver them to his friends. He had been retired a long time, so I knew this was a labor of sacrificial love and we appreciated it all the more because of it.

One day he called from Georgia, stranded when his car broke down. Would Dan come and get him? Not a second thought. Before we knew it, Dan was on the road to bring our friend back home. He drove from central Florida to Georgia and back. With or without the friend's car, I don't remember. For Dan, it was no sacrifice.

On another occasion, a young couple who had moved to our area from South Florida, were visiting friends there when the husband had some kind of life-threatening respiratory attack. He couldn't breathe. My friend, Jane, who was an RN and was working at a hospital on the west coast, said she had seen several young men come in with the same symptoms and a few died before they ever reached ICU. The young wife was pleading for prayer. My husband, the hero, grabbed his "cape," mounted his faithful Harley and left immediately for many miles south. Dan didn't speak any Spanish and the farther south you go in Florida, the fewer "English speaking" people there are. He had never been to that area, so just asking for directions was complicated. But he eventually found the hospital and Doug, visited him and prayed for him. Leaving the results to God, he said his good byes and returned home within 24 hours. What a champion! God did His work, and healed Doug. They returned home whole and happy.

The mother of a long time friend learned she had cancer and the end result of her treatment was having to wear a colostomy bag. Not good. There were lots of disasters in the changing, etc and my friend spent a lot of hours helping her. It has been over a year and the devastation has taken its toll on them all. But love sacrifices. It is a life of sacrifice and my friend is walking it out. She is blessed to have her mother still with her and she knows anything she can do for her is worth it.

One of the friends mentioned in the "friends" chapter, lives with her pastor husband who has an unbelievable sacrificial walk with the Lord. They live in the cold of Montana, and opened a Church where there had been none, alongside an Indian reservation. Now, many years later, using a wheelchair and suffering much pain, he continues to preach Jesus Christ, and Him crucified, with the help of those who will get him into the Church and behind the pulpit. The interesting thing is, I don't think he considers his lifestyle a sacrifice. His wife, my friend, is unbelievable in her ministry to those around her, and those she reaches out to, miles and miles away. She truly sends the gospel to the uttermost ends of the earth. Through her unusual ministry, she "found" me. And we have been friends and prayer partners ever since.

The phone woke us at 2:30 am. I had gotten used to reminding Dan that it was [always] "his call." "Hey, Dan," our friend Tor slurred, "I messed up." Like everyone, Tor loved Dan and felt he could call him at any time, day or night, for anything at all. "Dan, I ate some weird mushrooms and now I am so sick. Can you help me?"

Dan held the phone to one ear as he began dressing. "Where are you, Tor?" he asked. "Okay, okay. I'm coming. I'll be there in a minute. Don't go anywhere," he continued.

At that point, Dan was dressed and out the door to find the lost puppy. Tor had mental problems, drug problems, family problems, and anything else you could think of.

Later that morning, I learned "the rest of the story." While driving, Dan asked the Lord for the antidote. He surely had no idea what to do. The Lord told him to get Tor to drink as much milk as he could get down. He did and the end result was an exhausted but happy Tor and surely, a happy pastor. Sleepy, but happy.

Probably the most sacrificial *lifestyle* began after Dan passed away. During the forty plus years after Chip's birth, I had never been to a hospital for any reason. But then the physical walls began to tumble down around me. Chip and his family made the decision to move from Citrus County to Spring Hill to live close by and care for me. They sold their house and moved in with me while they continued to look for a home in this area. By then, he had accepted the position as pastor in the Church Dan founded. Not long after they had settled in, I had an emergency situation that called for paramedics rushing into the house and wiggling me onto a gurney to transport me to the hospital. It was a critical condition with a phenomenal loss of blood.

Chip found the perfect house just around the corner from mine, which made the "Help! I've fallen!" calls more "convenient." He and Zuzana insisted I keep my cell phone with me at all times. I have it hanging around my neck right now.

A series of emergency circumstances began. "Help! I've fallen and I can't get up!"—is no longer humorous to me. It seems for months, literally, I was falling. Chip got used to the words, "I've fallen again . . . ." Each time, it was critical. It all began when I attempted to transplant some shrubbery close to the house. I pulled on the plant, falling backwards, and slammed into a faucet protruding from the outside wall. That caused a huge bruised and painful area from under one breast and across my back to the other breast. It took a while for the black and blue area to heal and the pain to leave. Another call followed a trip over a board on the cement floor of the garage. My thoughtful husband had placed a 2x4 to stop my car from striking the freezer. Again, it was, "Help, Chip! I've fallen and . . . ." Again, Chip rushed to my aid. He got many of those calls—day and night—and he was faithful, like his father—to come sacrificially and quietly to my aid.

He and Zuzana were at my house one evening when I tripped over something and slammed into the corner of a wall—causing a bloody mess of my face and a huge black eye. Surprisingly, I never heard any "comments" *from anyone* about the fact that I was constantly covered with bumps and bruises.

A year ago, I was again working in the yard, pulling weeds, and I fell face forward hitting my head on the cement sidewalk. I heard a "crack" and blood gushed; I made "the call." When Chip drove up, he said my head had swollen to twice its size and blood was everywhere. We went to the hospital and I never looked in the mirror. It was sufficient o see the shocked looks on faces of everyone who entered the room. There were gasps as people saw me for the first time. My granddaughters were horrified and hid behind their parents. I was in the hospital for almost a week and today I still have an enlarged place on my forehead. I don't work in t he year anymore.

Following the falls, I began losing large amounts of blood. Calls to Chip began another series of trips to the hospital and weekly stays. After a few of those, I was diagnosed with cancer. After the diagnosis, I experienced a real peace. I felt the Lord speak to me and remind me not to entertain fear, but to rest in Him. It came easy.

After chemo and radiation, I've had two confirming reports that the cancer is gone. I'm sure Chip is sleeping better. I'm gaining strength as we speak and I haven't fallen in over a year. Is God good for what?? Yesterday, i spent some time with my neighbor, a sweet widow who told me how good I looked. I thought about it. Several people had mentioned the same thing. I didn't know how I'd changed or what made me "look better." But I'm grateful for each positive step I'm taking in this recovery. It's all God.

CHAPTER TWENTY-FOUR

The Passion of Another New Beginning

I woke up one morning recently and suddenly felt a refreshing in my spirit. It was as though I had a new lease on life: like I had taken a deep breath—inhaling it into the depths of my spirit.

Today I had lunch with the melodious duet of Luciano Pavarotti and Celine Dion in the background. Can it get mulch better than that? The richness of Pavarotti's tenor brought the vision of his big grin as he belted out one refrain after another. Passion. His was a passion that was not only wonderful to hear but visually thrilling. You knew he loved not only the music itself but the ability to reach to the heavens with that God given gift. I was thrilled to learn *he began singing in his Church choir as a youngster.*

What a difference to see and hear a talent so passionate it causes others to pale in comparison. Pavarotti held some concerts in various countries with pop singers joining him in duets. Many of the popular young vocalists received ovations as they tackled the difficult compositions. And Pavarotti loved every minute of it. That's what made his music so delightful to *watch.* You knew he loved it and loved doing it. He gave himself *passionately* to each delivery.

"The report" was a shocker. The cancer had appeared in my liver and lungs. There was no gasp. No "catch in my throat." It was just a fact. God's comforting word was still good: "don't entertain fear, don't get in a hurry about anything." To me, that meant, "prioritize. Get things done that need to be done." Completing this book is at the top of the list. In order to have a legacy—it has to be completed and "left." I sought the Lord, "How can this be "a beginning" at this point in my life?"

The next chapter in my life promises to be one of true passion. A conclusion of the passions that have built up over a lifetime. The crescendo of angel's anthems. I sense the heavens opening up and heaven's choirs filling the universe with love's passion.

Several times during the years I have been blessed to be "near" the witnessing of angelic hosts, the sounds of heavenly choirs, etc. While in the same room, at church one night, children were playing in a corner quietly and then, when the "service" was over, they calmly shared the visitation of a large angel who hovered over their group while the adults did their thing. "Wasn't he big, mom?" one child asked. But of course, the adults were not privy to that visitation. During a particularly anointed time of worship one Sunday morning, Dan and I looked at each other, knowingly. We had both heard the enormous angelic chorus right there in the midst of our 50+ congregation, with swelling sounds of glory. Breathtaking glory.

I walked into the sanctuary after a bathroom run and was shocked to see, in the midst of glorious praise, smoke settling over the congregation. No one else seemed to see it. Yet, there it was. It didn't "stay" long, but soon, quietly vanished. The setting: we were renting a community center on Sunday mornings, usually following some kid of Saturday night party with all the accompanying "goo." We had to go in on Sunday morning, scrub down the sticky residue of beer, etc., take down or set up tables, sound equipment, etc. all before beginning the meeting. Wonderful way to start the day. We felt blessed to have a meeting place.

As I review the passions relived in this book, I'm aware of little "seeds" bursting into buds. I know that even now they are forming new passions—of creativity, of music, of art, of love and compassion, so many ready to yield all that they have.

I remember the first time I experienced that explosion of pure passion. I had recently received the baptism of the Holy Spirit and one day I felt overwhelmed by God's powerful love. It poured in to my spirit—deeper and deeper—until I finally expressed my inability to contain it. "No more! No more! I can not hold any more!" I gasped, as His love filled my heart to overflowing. That was truly passion at its uttermost. I never experienced that depth again, but have always maintained that sweet memory.

When I fell in love with my husband, I heard myself say over and over, "I love you soooo much!" I never stopped, but was always surprised at the depth of our love for each other. I realized a dream had come true when I became conscious that I would spent the rest of my life waking up next to this man I loved so much. I knew that our love was locked in our passion for Jesus, and the three fold cord held fast all our married life.

We flew to Alaska to be at the birth of a granddaughter, prayed with the daughter in law with each contraction, and held that tiny being just moments after her arrival. What a thrill!

Words spoken that soared through my spirit," Gramma!" No sound so powerful!

Lily stood next to her dad in their home and sang, "Come, Now is the time to worship." Grampa and I were visiting. It was a thrill.

Letters from around the world from David—enough to say, "I'm thinking of you, Mom!" Warm rushes to my heart.

Phone calls when I needed a lift—hysterical laughs as Craig went on and on . . . . What a boost to my spirit!

Last Sunday I experienced a passionate thrust as my seven year old granddaughter gently walked to the front of the Church. My son played the guitar and quietly sang a worship song, and Hannah began an interpretive dance. Not a dry eye. I, again, was overwhelmed.

I've lived a life of passion and become conscious of it with every memory.

Again, my heart aches for those who live mundane lives, never experiencing what I've talked to you about. I don't know how to tell you to "get there," but I do encourage you to get to "know Jesus"—choose to draw close to him and don't let go until you have reached the depth of His love. He promises to meet you there.

When you meet Him, you'll understand what passion is.

Laura and Paul Savage
(Geri's Parents)

Geri Cole at the Tampa Florida Police Department

Officer Dan Cole at the Tampa Police Department, 1965

Dan and Geri Cole on their Wedding Day

Geri Cole on Her Wedding Day

Dan and Geri Cole Going on a Motorcycle Ride

Dan and Geri Cole Enjoying Lunch at their Church